THE FALLACIES OF BLACK CAPITALISM

A Thesis Presented to the Faculty of the Graduate School Pace College

In Partial Fulfillment of the Requirements for the Degree Master of Business Administration

CHARLES G. WELLS
AUGUST 1972

PAGE PUBLISHING
Conneaut Lake, PA

First originally published by Page Publishing 2022

ISBN 978-1-6624-6513-0 (pbk)
ISBN 978-1-6624-6515-4 (digital)

Printed in the United States of America

To Joyce Jones Wells, my babe

Contents

LIST OF TABLES

CHAPTER 1

Introduction

The slogan "Black Capitalism" is not new. Blackowned businesses in America have a history that extends back to the colonization of the United States, yet Black businesses have not developed to any significant extent since then.

Statement of the problem

When one studies the history of the Black man's role in American business, one soon discovers that the status of Black business has declined. Instead of growing and developing from generation to generation, Black business has stagnated in a cycle of frustration.

Black Americans have suffered because they have been denied the right to participate in the economic mainstream, and their confidence in their ability to learn and develop their business skills has been impeded by prejudice.

The effects of racism have left a terrible mark on the Black man, as well as the White; it has divided the nation and created an atmosphere of mistrust and hatred that must be overcome if this country is to survive economically and socially.

It was Calvin Coolidge who said, "The business of America is business." This is no mere philosophical generalization. Any student of American history knows the relationship between business and the Federal Government has always been an intimate one. One does not have to look to recent Federal legislation; all that is required is a casual study of the nation's economic history.

It has only been recently that the Federal Government has shown active concern with small business and even more recently with minority business.

The changes that have taken place in society and business over the years make it increasingly difficult for smaller businesses to survive. This is a fact that has hurt the Black man in his struggle to succeed in business.

It is in this context that this paper attempts to examine the program of Black Capitalism as a viable instrument of bringing Black people into the economic mainstream of America.

The problem

Purpose of the Study: The purpose of this paper is to examine the theme of Black Capitalism and its implications on American society as a whole. The study is designed to show why the problems attendant upon the presently constituted Black Capitalism programs will fail. To this end, the paper will attempt to:

1. Discuss the origin of Black Capitalism and its effect on the program.
2. Discuss the reasons why the program as designed will not succeed in making the kind of impact on the economy to give minorities a fair share in the system.
3. Explain the role of the Black church and Black university if Black Capitalism is to become a reality.
4. Discuss how the economic system of the ghetto will play a vital role in the success or failure of Black Capitalism.
5. Discuss the role of Corporate America in making Black Capitalism a reality.
6. Explain why the concept of Black Capitalism must achieve success.

Importance of the Study: The theme of Black Capitalism has been debated by proponents for and against the program which was designed to assist minorities in becoming a part of the mainstream of the American business community. The rhetoric has been overwhelming on both sides to the extent that some of the major issues have been beclouded.

There is a growing feeling among Black leaders and the masses of Black people that if Black people are to become an independent race of people, they must develop political and economic power.

Since the start of the Civil Rights movement, particularly with the impact of Black power advocates, economic advancement has been recognized as one of the most important dimensions. There is a new mood among Black people with respect to economic equality. Black people are saying that they want their rightful share of the American economy.

For twenty-two million Black Americans, the slogan, "equal opportunity," is an empty statement. For most Americans, economic advancement in business means participation. Historically, participation in business has denied Blacks through one means or another. Business has used such techniques as using tests to deny Blacks admittance to the skilled trade unions such as the steamfitters', the plumbers', and the sheet metal workers' unions.

Business has also used such excuses as that their clients or customers would not accept a Black or minority in sales. This technique has been used by many companies to keep Blacks from gaining positions in their marketing and sales departments.

The educational system has also contributed to keeping Blacks out of business. Black students traditionally have been counseled to enter such fields as teaching, the ministry, and medicine, but high school and college counselors have consistently advised Black students against studying business or entering programs for business. True, this advice may have been sound because the door to industry was closed, but this type of counseling has created an atmosphere of distrust and apathy in the Black community. Industry has also used such methods as hiring Blacks and placing them in positions they are either underqualified for or programmed to fail.

In a technological and information-oriented economy, education is an increasingly crucial resource. Yet this valuable resource has been used too often and hurt the Blacks' chances of advancement.

Another form of exclusion was the use of an arrest record to deny an individual a job, and since most Black people in the ghetto have had contact with the law at one time or another, this method denied a great number of Blacks jobs.

Black Americans are now seeking to become a part of this economic mainstream, but one must face reality and recognize that Black Capitalism will fail unless drastic changes are made in the development of the program and Blacks obtain the same opportunities to develop their business skills as Whites.

Entrepreneurship, while it has considerable emotional appeal, is not always a practical solution. A major problem facing the development of an effective program of "Black Capitalism" is a lack of business acumen and knowledge.

Traditionally, through racism and other forms of exclusion, such as union participation and hiring practices, Blacks have been denied participation in business for so long that there is no business tradition in the Black community from which young people can learn the rules of the game.

Black America has to ask itself some very important questions. Is the capitalistic system capable of eradicating ghettos, inferior schools, of providing equality of opportunity? Many Blacks, the author included, strongly feel that the economics of the country has to undergo essential changes through political action, or we can never hope to destroy racism and develop the necessary skills to create a strong Black business community.

America is facing a serious crisis. It is going through a phase where its values and traditions are being questioned and in some quarters, i.e., the Panthers, the Black Muslims, and the Weathermen are being totally rejected. Blacks are becoming more involved in politics and seeking community control of their schools and are making a serious effort to drive out those individuals who exploit the inhabitants of the ghetto.

"Black Capitalism" is not a new approach to bringing business into the Black community. It is an old idea in new clothing. Marcus Garvey, a British West Indian, an advocate of "Back to Africa," first called for development of business in the community as long ago as 1923, as a part of his program of Black separatism.

The term "Black Capitalism" is misleading and confusing. Capitalism does not vary according to the color of its practitioners. Whether in Watts or on Wall Street, capitalism develops according to certain time-honored rules and principles. It is created out of know-how, hard work, saving, and intelligent risk-taking. It cannot be given ready-made to anyone nor can it be legislated. At the same time, though, would-be capitalists and entrepreneurs in the ghettos *urgently* need the help of experienced White businessmen.

They need financial assistance as well as managerial guidance.

It seems difficult to comprehend why in a country as rich as ours that so many people are living in poverty and are excluded from the money-making enterprises of this wealthy country, yet one has to face the hard realities that racism and greed have been effective tools in denying Blacks and other minorities the possibility of succeeding in business.

Author Theodore Cross has written: "The dangers to America are too great to permit 163 ghettos to continue to build with impoverished Blacks at the rate of five hundred thousand people a year." [1]

In the preamble to the Economic Opportunity Act of 1964, it states, "The policy of the United States is to eliminate poverty." If this policy is to become a reality, then Blacks, other minorities, and the poor must be given an opportunity to participate in the economic system.

The late Whitney Young Jr., former National Executive Director of the National Urban League, used to tell how he marveled at the creativity of the White economy, however distorted, which has consistently and effectively excluded Blacks from participating in executive and blue-collar jobs. It is this creativity on the part of the White business community that has brought about the lack of business development in the Black community.

If America is ever really to become the land of opportunity, it must create a viable enterprise system in the Black community and other minority communities. Business must use its resources to develop the talent necessary for minority enterprise to grow and flourish. "Black Capitalism" must become more than a slogan; it must be

---

[1] Theodore L. Cross, *Black Capitalism* (New York: Atheneum, 1969), p. VII.

replaced with minority enterprises that can compete in a competitive economy.

Scope and Limitations of the Study: The scope of this study is concerned with the concept that Black Capitalism will not have any impact on changing the economic conditions of Blacks and other minorities in this country. The author will attempt to show the importance of the involvement of big business and that a change in attitude is necessary to achieve any degree of success.

This study shall be limited to the current literature on the subject of Black Capitalism, resource literature relating the role of slavery and early Black history to the present problem, and personal interviews with Black businessmen.

The research for this paper covers a period of four years of investigating literature, discussions with Blacks in the field, and the author's experience in the field. This paper will not attempt to propose solutions to the problems of racism, of segregated schools, or the urban problem as it relates to the Black community. It is the author's purpose to discuss the inequities of the program of Black Capitalism and to offer possible solutions based upon a study of the problems and the author's experience.

Hypothesis: The hypothesis to be tested in this study is as follows:

That Black Capitalism will not succeed unless new approaches are developed to provide minorities with managerial skills.

Method of Testing the Hypothesis: The hypothesis will be tested by comparing the findings of various other authors with the author's experience while working in the field of economic development.

Method of Research: The major portion of the methodological approach to this paper centered around the use of the books, papers, periodicals, and other professional literature presently available dealing with the subject of Black Capitalism. This information has been coupled with interviews with Black businessmen, Civil Rights workers, Black entrepreneurs, Blacks working in the field of economic development, and the author's firsthand experiences in economic development.

Definition of Key Terms

The major terms used in the text are as follows:

Black Capitalism—The strategy which urges creation of new jobs and profit centers inside ghetto areas. The program also seeks to transfer the ownership of ghetto business from White to Black control, at the same time, building in the ghetto new banks, insurance companies, production, and service facilities. Today, Black Capitalism is an insignificant force in America.

Black Life Insurance Industry—This is the only significant element of Black Capitalism in America today. The Black insurance industry showed dramatic growth before 1950 when the low life expectancy of Negroes insulated the Black life insurance companies from White competition. Since 1963, Black life insurance companies' assets have grown at an average annual rate of 3 percent, compared to 9.5 percent for the industry as a whole. Although this industry is the only form of Black enterprise (other than ghetto banks) to employ substantial elements of capital in commerce, these companies have assets of only 0.2 percent of the industry total. The largest Negro-controlled life company, North Carolina Mutual Life of Durham, North Carolina, has assets of $90 million, about 1/300th of the size of Prudential Life in Newark.[2]

Business Survival—The view that it is impossible to maintain a healthy growing total business economy in a nation so long as large numbers of people in the society are poor. Its proposal that business solutions to the urban crises are necessary conditions of business survival is the foundation for current ghetto programs of the National Alliance of Businessmen. The theory of "essential business survival" seriously retards Federal incentive programs to build business and commerce. In the ghetto, the strategy incorrectly assumes that the inherent threat of the urban crises contains within itself an adequate motivating force to persuade businessmen to move forward with ghetto-enrichment programs, which fosters the development of minority business.[3]

Buy Black—An old slogan urging Blacks to utilize their economic consumer power by purchasing only through Black-owned shops, Black entrepreneurs, and Black producers.

Capitalism—An economic system characterized by private or corporate ownership of capital goods by investments that are determined by private decision rather than

---

[2] Ibid., p. 212.
[3] Ibid.

by state control and by prices, production, and the distribution of goods that are determined in a free market.

Chance to Fail—The theory that Blacks will never "make it" in business unless they are given an opportunity to compete on equal terms with the White entrepreneur. It ignores the unassailable facts that desegregation and the resulting new White competition for Black patronage have: (1) caused the total number of Black businesses to shrink by 20 percent between 1950 and 1960; (2) severely reduced the growth rate of Black insurance companies; and (3) caused wholesale failures during the past decade of Black service establishments such as funeral and nursing homes, dry cleaners, grocery stores, and hotels.

Charity in the Ghetto—The businessman's need to "do his part" and simply share his wealth with the ghetto poor rather than share his knowledge of how to grow rich.

CORE—The Congress of Racial Equality is one of the principal Black groups moving aggressively to build Black entrepreneurship. CORE was one of the architects of the Community Self-Determination Bill submitted to Congress in 1968 with the backing of twenty-five US senators. This bill would set up community-development corporations in poverty areas to acquire, create, and manage all business in their areas.

Entrepreneur—One who organizes, manages, and assumes the risks of a business or enterprise.

Entrepreneurial Segregation—The protective commercial monopoly formerly enjoyed by the ghetto service business.

Freedmen's Banks—A system of Black-owned-and-controlled banks established after the Civil War. Most of the Freedmen's Bank units failed in the panics and the depressions of the past seventy-five years.

Leverage—The use of borrowed money and senior equity, in combination with risk capital, to magnify the value of an initial stake. The technique of leverage is a common route to wealth or affluence in the normal economy. The ghetto economy almost never uses leverage to acquire (or magnify the value of) real estate or capital goods.

Riot—An ineffective method of communicating the real economic needs of the ghetto to the main economy.

Risk Capital—The wealth-building process of generating discretionary income and converting it into venture capital for commitment to a business opportunity. This is almost totally lacking in the ghetto economy.

Blanket Guarantee—The short-form loan guarantee procedure developed by the Small Business Administration in 1968 to expedite approval of SBA guarantees of minority business loan applications.

Blocked-Opportunity Theory—The theory that riots are a consequence of the prolonged exclusion of Negroes from the social and economic benefits enjoyed by the main economy.

Small Business Administration—An agency of the Federal Government established to finance and assist small businessmen in America. The program has been plagued by red tape, onerous bureaucratic procedures, and inadequate appropriations from the Congress.

Soft Loans—A retail or commercial credit extended in the ghetto economy to a Black borrower whose credit profile is considered unbankable. The soft loan is, in reality, a charitable gift, except that it is not deductible for tax purposes until it fails and is written off against the lender's bad-debt reserve.

Ghetto Business Monopoly—The immunity enjoyed by ghetto businesses from White competition. Since 1950, attitudes favoring social integration and new laws banning discrimination against Blacks have opened up the entire economy to Black patronage. The monopoly which was formerly assured to ghetto hotels, banks, life insurance companies, and restaurants has all but disappeared.

Jobs Now—A nationwide private business effort to put Blacks in jobs. It has failed to give the necessary emphasis to an expansion of the employment capabilities of the ghetto economy.

Freedom National Bank—The largest Black-controlled bank in America, with its principal office in West Harlem and one branch in the Bedford-Stuyvesant ghetto of Brooklyn. Freedom National Bank has assets of $27 million, and in size, ranks 1,733[th] among banks in the United States.

Ghetto—A quarter of a city in which members of a minority group or disadvantaged live because of social, legal, or economic pressure.

Ghetto-nomics—A term used by Blacks working in the field of economic development to describe the economy of the ghetto.

Ghetto-Marketplace—The market system serving low-income neighborhoods.

Marcus Garvey—A native of Jamaica who founded a separatist movement in the United States. He was deported to his homeland.

MESBIC—A program started by the Nixon administration. The term means Minority Enterprise Small Business Investment Company (MESBIC).

White Power Structure—A term used by Blacks to describe the business and government system that runs this country.

Organization of remainder of the study

The remainder of the thesis consists of the following:

Chapter 2 discusses the history of the Black man's bondage and the effect slavery had on the Black American. The relationship of slavery and the crisis that Black business is facing today is examined. The attitude of the church during slavery is also viewed to show the relationship between the Judeo-Christian doctrine and the condition of the Black American.

In Chapter 3, the economy of the ghetto is examined to show the effect this subeconomy has on the development of Black Capitalism. The attitude of the Black community toward Black Capitalism will also be discussed to understand a major problem facing the development of a viable system of Black enterprise.

Chapter 4 discusses the role of the Black university and the Black church in the development of Black Capitalism.

The Black church study is made to show the leadership role it has played in the Black community and its relationship to Black Capitalism. A case study in Black Capitalism is also analyzed to point up some of the problems facing the minority entrepreneur.

Chapter 5 centers around the role corporate America must play if Black Capitalism is to become more than a slogan. Recommendations will also be discussed in this section. The problems created by business will also be analyzed in the hope that some solution might be offered. The "MESBICS" concept will also be discussed in this section.

Chapter 6 presents a summary.

Chapter 2

Historical View of Black Capitalism

To understand the crisis in which the Black entrepreneur finds himself, one must examine the origin of slavery and its effect on the Black man in today's society.

Slavery had existed in all parts of the world during the seventeenth and eighteenth centuries. During this period, it was as prevalent in South America as it was in the United States. However, compared with slavery that existed in South America, the scars upon the Black man in North America were unusually deep since the United States did not recognize slaves as human beings.

This raises a psychological point that remains valid today: Because the Negro was "different" in appearance, many Whites justified their different treatment of him. That the vast majority of Negroes were non-Christians in a proclaimed Christian land added another rationalization for slavery. In North America, Black slaves were treated as property, a capital good the same as an animal, other chattel, or a machine today. Such treatment of the slaves denied the very essence of the Judea-Christian traditions with its insistence on the infinite worth of every human being.

Slavery in South America recognized that every human being had a soul and some freedom. This freedom involved the right to own and inherit property. Thus any slave could work his way to complete freedom and could also inherit property from his legal forebears.

In the North American colonies, however, to protect the economic interest of the slave holder, many artificial means of bondage were employed to maintain the economic institution of slavery. Slave masters had many children, but the American social definition of a Negro, which encompassed "anyone with Negro ancestry," had to be instituted for the survival of the American economic system. Thus any one of the progeny from interracial contacts was automatically classified as Negro and could not inherit property.

There are those who believe that "White perceptions of Negroes, and the historical inculcation of the perceptions in the minds of Negroes themselves, are at the root of our present troubles."[4] Unquestionably, slavery with its dehumanizing effects on both Blacks and Whites is important. It is the individual racist who perpetuates the institutions which deny equal rights to Blacks and other minority groups. Men are shaped by their upbringing, by the institutional environment in which they mature.

---

[4] Senator Fred R. Harris, Foreword, in William H. Grier and Price M. Cobbs, *Black Rage* (New York: Bantam, 1968), p. VIII.

Attitudes were formed and ideologies constructed to fulfill the selfish interests of individuals and groups, i.e., the slave master in the seventeenth and eighteenth centuries.

These attitudes may assume a life of their own, but they are spawned of special needs. As Grier and Cobbs have written, "Slavery required the creation of a particular kind of person, one compatible with a life of involuntary servitude. The ideal slave had to be absolutely dependent and have a deep consciousness of personal inferiority... Teachings so painstakingly applied do not disappear easily."[5]

The White slave master had to justify the place of the slaves; they were children who had to be cared for. This attitude is prevalent among Whites in our present day society. "A modern version holds that Black people are little different from other citizens save for a paucity of education and money. The reason for these deficiencies is left vague."[6] The weight of slavery has had a lasting effect on the Black man in America, yet the first Blacks to arrive in the Western Hemisphere were not the twenty slaves traded in Jamestown Harbor by a Dutch captain in 1619. The first Blacks to come to this country were free men such as "Pedro Alonzo Nino, who was the navigator of the Nina, one of the ships Christopher Columbus sailed to the New World in 1492. Neflo de Olana was among thirty Negroes serving with Balboa when the Spanish explorer discovered the Pacific Ocean."[7] There were other Black men who came to this land as heroes. For example, Estevan, a Negro scout

---

[5] Grier and Cobbs, *Black Rage*, pp. 20–21.

[6] Ibid., p. 2.

[7] C. Eric Lincoln, *The Negro Pilgrimage in America* (New York, Bantam, 1967), p.2.

for the explorer Narraez, was the first non-Indian to penetrate what is now Arizona.

A rationale for slavery

With such a noble and heroic beginning, how did the Black man become a slave and spend two hundred and fifty years in a condition of bondage that would affect Blacks down to the present day?

Initially, slaves were not identified with any particular race or group of people. The earliest known slaves became slaves by virtue of being prisoners of war. Slavery, as with all social customs, underwent changes in style. At first, prisoner-slaves were held as the property of a victorious state. Later, with the advent of the slave markets, individual ownership of slaves became one of the first "status symbols." In Europe, the fourth and fifth centuries saw serfdom replace the former practice of chattel slavery. Serfs were peasants "bound to the land" of their lords and worked without pay. The serf enjoyed an advantage over the chattel slave by being attached permanently to one family, enabling the serf to keep his own family intact.

The Middle Ages saw a new rationale for slavery come into existence in the form of religious differences. Christians were enslaved by Moslems and Christians enslaved Moslems and other non-Christians.

The English colonies, desperate for labor needed to push inland to clear the forests and cultivate the land, attempted to use and enslave Indians for this task. "The Indians proved unadaptable for this type of work, and many died in the fields." They were killed by the English because they refused to work. The search for labor then focused upon White Englishmen who were brought to the colonies as indentured servants or "bondsmen."

These bondsmen were taken from debtors' prisons, and some were convicted felons. Many poor Englishmen, eager to escape the repressive class structure of their homelands, signed contracts in return for passage to America. Bondsmen were not chattels in the same sense as were slaves. It should be noted, however, that bondsmen could be (and often were) traded and sold to new holders. When the supply of voluntary indentured bondsmen began to dwindle, a new source of labor had to be found.

The importation of Negro bondsmen dates from 1619, when twenty Negroes were purchased from a Dutch ship. It should be noted that those twenty human beings came to the colonies as bondsmen, not as slaves. Under then existing English law, a slave had no legal status; he could not sue, be sued, or give testimony. English law provided that persons who had been baptized became enfranchised. Many slaves converted to Christianity in hopes of becoming freed men. It was not until 1682 that the Virginia Law reduced all non-Christians, including later converts to permanent slave status. This was the turning point in slavery in North America since the African slaves brought to this country against their will were non-Christians.

The role of the church

In the colonies of the feudal and despotic Spanish and Portuguese empires of South America, the Catholic Church asserted its vested interest in the souls of the slaves.

Since marriage is a sacrament, slaves had to be married in the Church in South America. Once married, the slaves could not be separated, and slave owners were required to give their slaves religious instruction.

One major difference between the slave systems of North America and South America was that the slaves of South America had laws to protect them against mistreatment by their owners. To enforce these laws, each colony had an official protector of the slave, known variously as the syndic, procurator, or attorney general.

This type of "open system" permitted a relatively smooth transition from slavery to freedom. South American law viewed slavery as a misfortune that could happen to anyone and because it insisted that slaves had a soul and mind, the opprobrium the colonies attached to color never developed.

Another important factor was that South American Whites never seriously maintained that a Negro slave was incapable of being free. Freed slaves in South America enjoyed the same legal rights as Whites and, on the whole, the same social status. The result of this type of slave system was that the "Sambo" tradition never took root in South America.

Slavery in the colonies developed in such a way as to convince the Whites that Africans were inherently inferior and incapable of freedom. Equally important, the system of slavery was administered so as to make the Negroes behave as if they were inferiors—to distort their personalities and crush their mentalities in such a way as to make them in fact incapable of utilizing the "freedom" that finally became theirs after two and a half centuries of bondage.

Slavery took its peculiar and cruel form in the English colonies precisely because there was no precedent either in tradition or in common law.

The English colonies saw slavery as unnatural and had to find a way to justify putting men into bondage. The colonist solved this dilemma with the rationale that since the Africans were inferior, they lacked the capacity to be free men.

Malcolm X, in a speech before his death, stated this fact most forcibly when he said, "The worst crime the White man has committed has been to teach us to hate ourselves."

The conditions imposed on the slaves by the English colonies were frequently ignored by the churches, although some denominations, notably the Unitarians, were consistently anti-slavery. Unlike the church in South America, which viewed slaves as humans and provided protection for them, this was not so in the colonies.

"In the early nineteenth century, the Methodist Church attacked slavery as a moral blight upon America. But by 1836, the Methodists declared they had no right, wish, or intention of interfering in the civil and political relations between master and slave as it existed in the slave-holding states of the Union."[8]

---

[8] Ibid., p. 47.

The church in the colonies, for the most part, supported the system of slavery, whereas the church in South America helped the slaves and protected their right to be treated as human beings.

The traumatic experience of the Black American during that period of history in this country when slavery was at its peak has left serious scars on the Black community today.

Slavery became more prevalent than ever with the invention of the cotton gin. The economic base of the South was changed drastically by this invention, and since large numbers of workers were needed to keep the cotton gins running, there was an increased demand for slaves.

The South had more reason than ever to keep the slave system with this increased demand for cotton. The slave found himself caught even more hopelessly in the toils of oppression as greed became a motive.

Slavery did more than physical damage to the Black African, it stripped him of his dignity, identity, and cultural heritage. The psychological damage that the stigma of slavery left on the Black community and the brainwashing that Blacks are inferior is felt in the Black community today, and this feeling is still held by many Whites of the South and North.

The problems of self-awareness

The years of slavery and the suppression of the slaves' mental capacities have created a tremendous problem of self-awareness and identification among Blacks. Blacks have had many images of themselves. This is true of all people and groups. Every group tends to develop an image of itself that is marked by the greatest sense of worth and dignity. Until recently, the Black man in America has viewed himself without dignity and a sense of worth.

Blacks have been taught for so long that they are inferior, worthless, and are the nation's adolescents.

Dr. Nathan Wright Jr. has said:

> Negroes are a peculiarly American hybrid. But they have been taught to think of themselves in terms of the African portion of their ancestry alone. Although European and Indian by blood in part and chiefly European in terms of culture, Negroes have been forced to develop a self-image which reflects a primary identification with their peculiarly African past. Thus the American Negro's initial self-image was associated with his experiences on African soil and his inferior conditions of slavery.[9]

Slavery has left an indelible mark on race relations in America that affects the behavioral patterns of both White and Black in today's society. America, from its inception, has been a land of opportunity and hope for the insecure and the dispossessed. The first colonists and subsequent

---

[9]   Nathan Wright Jr., *Black Power and Urban Unrest* (New York: Hawthorn Books, 1967), pp. 157–58.

immigrants were, for the most part, frustrated economically, politically, or socially. The spirit of America can be generalized as being the spirit of the insecure and frustrated coming to grips with a vast new land, rich beyond their hopes, and attempting to obtain through the exploitation of every opportunity in this new land, the security previously denied them in Europe. Dr. Kenneth Clark states that:

> Black slavery was a form of security obtained through the subjugation and humiliation of human beings. It singled out human beings who were perceptibly different physically, who for the most part were nonChristian in religion, who spoke a different language and, in general, had a quite different cultural background. For these reasons, it was easy and convenient to look down upon them, exploit them, treat them as inferior beings without guilt feelings.[10]

Economic greed has been cited as one of the major reasons why slavery became so powerful in the early history of our country.

The approval of the Protestant Church was another leading reason that slavery became entrenched in American culture. The role of the church in the colonies was not pow-

---

[10] Kenneth B. Clark, "A Psychologist Looks at Dis crimination Patterns," *MBA*, Vol. 6 (January 1972) p. 34.

erful enough to exert the same influence on the people as the church in South America, and church laws were not as defined in the Protestant Church as in the Catholic faith. The church's approval of slavery is a black mark on religious institutions that will not be completely erased in this country. This same attitude toward Blacks by the church can be observed in some sections of the country today.

Effects of slavery on Black economic development

Slavery has played a dominant role in preventing the Black American from developing a tradition of business know-how in this country. The question is often asked, how is it that other ethnic groups, such as the Jewish people and Italians, became prosperous in business?

One argument is "that this situation exists because Blacks are arriving in the cities at a time when opportunities for the establishment of small businesses are on the decline."[11]

This may well be true, but the Black man's failure to achieve success as a businessman must certainly be attributed more centrally to racism. Eugene Foley supports this contention with this statement: "The culture has simultaneously unduly emphasized achievement in business as the primary symbol of success and has blindly developed or imposed an all-pervading racism that denied

---

[11] Nathan Glazer and Daniel P. Moynihan, *Beyond the Melting Pot* (Cambridge, Mass.: The MIT Press and Harvard University Press, 1963), p. 143.

the Black man the necessary opportunities for achieving this success."[12]

In most urban cities, ghetto business is dominated by Jewish merchants. An exception to this is in New Orleans, where the Black ghetto businesses are controlled by Italians. In all cases, hatred is aimed at the group which economically dominates the ghetto.

European immigrants had three major advantages over Blacks in obtaining a start in business. First, the immigrants usually had a sense of clannishness. Glazer and Moynihan point out that because of such group solidarity, funds were more readily available. "Those who had advanced themselves created little pools for ethnic businessmen and professionals to tap."[13] This has not been as true of Blacks until the present decade, when a sense of identification and group pride have developed among a sizable number of Blacks.

Second, there is the legacy of slavery. Blacks have not only the "badge of color but also the ingrained burden of generations of cultural and economic deprivations."[14]

The plantation system offered the Negro no experience with money, no incentive to save, no conception of time or progress—none of the basic experiences to prepare him for the urban money economy. Instead, it indoctrinated him to believe in his own inferiority, to be resigned, while it held him in the fold of a culture dominated by a spiritual, other-worldly, escapist outlook…[15]

---

[12] Eugene P. Foley, "The Negro Businessman: In Search of a Tradition," in Parsons and Clark, *The Negro American*, p. 572.

[13] Glazer and Moynihan, op. cit., p. 33.

[14] Jeanne R. Lowe, *Cities in a Race with Time* (New York: Vintage, 1967), p. 283.

[15] Ibid., p. 283.

This is a limited view of the effects of slavery. It ignored the "calculated cruelty designed to crush the spirit," the malice and the hatred which Blacks endured under slavery. Nor does such a view speak to the continuing record.

"When slavery ended and large-scale physical abuse was discontinued, it was supplanted by different but equally damaging abuse. The cruelty continued unabated in thoughts, feelings, intimidation, and occasional lynching. Black people were consigned to a place outside the human family and the whip of the plantation was replaced by the boundaries of the ghetto."[16]

Whether one blames the dominance of folk culture or at a more fundamental level, the limits slavery placed on Black development, it may be concluded that Blacks do lack "managerial skills and attitudes. Negroes as a race have been little exposed to business operations and lack technical experience and entrepreneurial values that are necessary for succeeding in business."[17]

A third and last factor, difficult to assess, is the importance of an economic base in some occupation or trade in which the group has a special advantage, a phenomenon not found among the Black population.

---

[16] Grier and Cobbs, op. cit., p. 20.

[17] Robert B. McKersie, "Vitalize Black Enterprise," *Harvard Business Review* (September–October 1968), 90.

Black Power

The rallying cry of "Black Power" was viewed by many leaders in the Black community as a positive slogan because it was a unifying element in the Black community.

Black Power was viewed as a first step for Black people to develop a sense of pride and dignity. It was the first time in the history of this country that the Black community was taking a stand and attempting to instill a feeling of worth and positiveness in its people. Psychologists foresaw this as an important first step in overcoming the inferior attitude that has prevailed among Blacks from the time of slavery.

The theme of Black Power is of great importance to both the Black and White community, as it seeks to bring about a new strength in the Black community.

Blacks, in the effort to develop this new sense of pride and dignity, must not forget that the cry of Black Power will not become a reality until the Black community develops a viable economic base and has "green power."

The slogan "Black Power" was received negatively in the White community because the meaning was misinterpreted to be that Blacks were going to use physical force to obtain their civil rights.

Civil rights and Black Power served a useful purpose in race relations in this country, for they provided a new dimension of dignity, pride, and sense of worth to the Black man, and it served to inform the White man that Blacks would no longer bow their heads and feel inferior to Whites because of their skin color. It was the beginning of a new era for the Black community, an era of developing a new inner strength and a sense of pride as a race of people.

It will take years to undo the shame of slavery or to erase from the minds of Black people the feelings that were instilled in them over the years, but it is an important first step.

Summary

The system of slavery that flourished in the colonies could not have become as strong as it did if the church had power similar to that of the Catholic Church in South America. One has to believe the church's lack of influence and the fact that slaves for the most part were non-Christians led to the brutal conditions that existed during slavery.

Slavery left a lasting mark on the mental attitude of the Black man and the White man in this country. Slavery created an attitude of superiority among the White race and a tradition of inferiority in the Black man.

True, slavery cannot be blamed completely for the crisis that exists today, but it played a major role in the development of a docile, timid Black community.

Slavery may no longer exist in its brutal form, but economic, educational, and political bondage still may be found in America today. If America is ever to realize its dream as a "land of opportunity," it must provide economic opportunity for its Black citizens.

CHAPTER 3

The Economic System of the Ghetto, Its Effects on the Development of Black Capitalism

Urbanologists and students of poverty have analyzed and written a great deal of descriptive material about the Black ghetto. Reports have detailed the extent of poverty, the number of families headed by women, the prevalence of substandard housing, the inferior quality of education, and the high rate of unemployment. The volumes of reports have not, however, been incorporated into a very satisfactory analysis of the causes which have created the ghetto, or the forces which perpetuate it.

Systematic discrimination has been cited as a major cause that sets off the van majority of Blacks from the rest of the working class. Economic oppression has been given as another cause that is used to keep Blacks a subclass of people.

The Black ghetto can best be viewed from the perspective of development economics. In relationships with the dominant White society, the Black ghetto stands as a unit apart, an internal colony exploited in a systematic fashion.

James Baldwin, the author, has noted that "Anyone who has ever struggled with poverty knows how extremely expensive it is to be poor."[18]

Baldwin was referring to the material and measurable cost to the poor in the marketplace. The author challenged any skeptical reader who doubted that the low-income consumer is at a disadvantage to "go shopping one day in Harlem—for anything—and compare Harlem prices and quality with those downtown…"[19]

The high price of being poor is, of course, only one aspect of the domestic crisis involving the ghetto inhabitant in the United States. Poverty in the ghetto has long been recognized and studied, but the economic system has generally been overlooked in terms of money generated in the ghetto community. Studies have shown that large sums of money exchange hands in the ghetto community, but very little is retained there to be used to improve the conditions of those living there.

Developmental view of the ghetto

Students of economics will find in the introductory chapters of standard development textbooks the following description of the typical underdeveloped country: "low

---

[18] James Baldwin, *Nobody Knows My Name* (New York: A Dell Book, 1964), p. 59.
[19] Ibid.

per capita income; high birth rate; a small, weak middle class; low rates of increase in labor productivity, capital formation, domestic savings; and a small monetized market."[20] The economy of such a country is heavily dependent on external markets where its few basic exports face an inelastic demand (that is, demand relatively constant regardless of price, and so expanding total output may not mean higher earnings).[21]

The economic system of the ghetto compared with White America closely parallels those between underdeveloped nations and the industrially advanced countries. The ghetto also has a relatively low per capita income, high birth rate, and high death rate. Ghetto residents are for the most part unskilled. Businesses that exist lack capital and managerial know-how. The incidence of credit default is high, and little saving takes place. What is saved is usually kept invested locally. Local markets are for the most part nonexistent. Goods and services tend to be "imported." For the most part, only the simplest and the most labor-intensive products are produced in the ghetto. The basic "export" of the ghetto is its unskilled labor power. The demand for this export does not increase to match the growth of the ghetto labor force. Ghetto businesses are owned in large part by non-ghetto residents, many of whom are White. Important jobs in the ghetto economy (teachers, policemen, postmen) are held by White outsiders. The Black ghetto is in many

---

[20] For example, see Everett E. Hagen, *The Economics of Development* (Homewood, Illinois: Richard D. Irwin, 1968), Part I.

[21] William K. Tabb, *The Political Economy of the Black Ghetto* (New York: W.W. Norton & Co. Inc., 197), p. 22.

ways in a position similar to that of the underdeveloped nation.

Whitney Young, the late Executive Director of the National Urban League, proposed that the government initiate a domestic "Marshall Plan" to aid the economic development of the ghetto community, similar to the plan used to assist underdeveloped countries of Europe.

Colonization Theory

The concept of viewing the ghettos of America as a colony to White America has also been fostered by Black militants like Malcolm X and Eldridge Cleaver.

That segregation existed in America for years has been acknowledged by Whites and Blacks alike. That job discrimination was pervasively clear but that such a relationship was colonial has been denied by Whites as well as some Black leaders.

Malcolm X and Eldridge Cleaver viewed the status of American Blacks to that of the subjugated dark-skinned around the world. They looked at America from the ghetto as outcasts, pronounced it racist, and declared that racism was part of the structure of America. Black militants saw the relation of White to Black in America as that of colonizers to colonized, oppressors to oppressed. Since a colonial relation is inherently unequal, it must be broken before one can talk integration.

There are two key relationships which must be proved to exist before a colonial analogy can be accepted: (1) economic control and exploitation, and (2) political dependence and subjugation. Both necessitate separation and inferior status. Urbanologists and social psychologists have long recognized that the ghetto is dependent and controlled by the White power structure. For the purpose of this paper, the author will attempt to analyze the relationship of economic control and exploitation as it relates to Black capitalism.

The term ghetto is defined for the purpose of this paper to be a quarter of a city in which members of a minority group or the disadvantaged live because of social, legal, or economic pressure.

Since America is a country that holds the achievement of material wealth to be important, economic oppression and exploitation has had a serious effect on the Black population which frequently judges one's success by the size of his home, automobile, and other possessions.

In our national concern for the alleviation of poverty and economic dependency, the need to know and understand what life looks like from the bottom of society is crucial. Meaningful change can be induced only if one understands the situation where one intends it to occur. It is unlikely, for example, that one can change or reduce rates of dependency and poverty without knowing the conditions of dependence to people caught up in them. Nor can one bring about a system of minority enterprise without knowing the quality of the existing problem of the economic systems of the ghetto.

The depression and the Black man

For one to understand the situation in which Black people in the ghetto find themselves today, it is important to examine the historical relationship between Blacks and Whites since the post-Civil War period. Blacks in this period were in an ambiguous economic position. It was during this time that racial strife became built into the social fabric, making joint action by poor Whites and Blacks extremely difficult.

"The free Blacks served the function of an equilibrating factor in the economy." They could hold jobs nobody else wanted, do the dirty work of the society, and be called upon for higher-paying jobs in periods of labor shortage. In slack periods, Blacks could be fired to make room for unemployed Whites. "Blacks were used as strike breakers in coal and iron mines, steel mills, lumber camps, meat-packing plants, and other industries."[22]

The depression caused Blacks to be pushed out of jobs that they had been recruited for during the labor shortage of World War I and the prosperity of the 1920s. Blacks were hit particularly hard because of the disastrous drop in agricultural earnings (especially cotton) and the loss of urban jobs to Whites.

The Black man in the ghetto still finds himself in a job cycle of frustration that keeps him on the bottom economic rung. The Black worker's place in the economy is

---

[22] Arthur M. Ross, *The Negro in the American Economy,* in *Employment, Race, and Poverty,* ed. Arthur M. Ross and Herbert Hill (New York: Harcourt, Brace & World, 1967), p. 12.

similar to that of the natives in the colony—he owns little and works at the lowest-paying job. The majority of Blacks seek work in a restricted labor market. Author Michael Piore has written:

> The manpower problems of the urban ghetto appear best defined in terms of a dual labor market: a primary market, and a secondary market, to which the urban poor are confined, decidedly less attractive, and in competition with welfare and crime.[23]

Ghetto labor market

The ghetto is a crazy complex of anomalies and paradoxes. Its economy borders on anarchy that defies all orderly roles of supply and demand. Gunnor Myrdal, the author, referred to this in *An American Dilemma* by saying: "The economic situation of Negroes in America is pathological. This inherent sickness of unpredictability in the Black economy is illustrated in all aspects of its feeble commerce."

"The paradoxical complexity of the ghetto is most visible in the important matter of jobs and unemployment. Basic to the high rate of ghetto unemployment is a paradoxical and equally high rate of unfilled job opportuni-

---

[23] Michael J. Piore, *Public and Private Responsibilities in On-the-Job Training of Disadvantaged Workers*, Department of Economics Working Paper, Number 23 (Cambridge, Mass.: The MIT Press, June 1968), pp. 2–3.

ties." Residents of the ghetto do not respond to the simple opportunity of a job. The ghetto poor do not line up at the employment gate because they believe it is a waste of time and they will not be hired. They are certain that, for Blacks, all jobs are dead-end jobs; unfortunately, history has proven this to be true for the most part.

The ghetto has a way of killing the motivation that caused Blacks to leave the rural areas of the South for the North with its higher wages and, later, on its higher welfare benefits.

"Once a Southern Black gets off the train at Chicago's Central Station and takes the five-dollar cab ride to Lawndale (his first encounter with the special tariffs of ghetto economics), his mobility and motivation end."[24] Southern Blacks, who left the rural areas of the South, like Mississippi, for the North encounter two phenomena that affected their chances to succeed. The first was the their encounter with the "special tariffs of ghetto economic, where everything cost, i.e., housing, food, etc. Since most of these individuals worked in low-paying jobs or had no jobs at all, this higher cost for everything had a tremendous negative impact on their lives.

The second major impediment to these individuals was they found themselves in an environment that they lacked the educational skills to succeed and that the White community was very hostile to their being in the city of Chicago. The type of hostility and anger that they experienced had a negative psychological effect on their ability to function and feel safe. Children stopped attending school

---

[24] Theodore L. Cross, *Black Capitalism* (New York: Atheneum, 1969), p. 22.

or playing in the streets of their communities, and adults stopped looking for work.

The White residents that they encountered on a daily basis took a page out the same terroristic playbook that groups like the KKK and other White nationalist groups used to instill fear in minority groups.

The ghetto environment with its complexities and oppressive nature has a way of destroying one's ambition to obtain an education.

In the ghetto economy, many factors interfere with a man's ability to obtain and hold a job. Ghetto residents are constantly faced with financial crises, like fighting off finance companies, eviction notices, bad credit, and the inability to meet rent payments. These conditions tend to interfere with an employee's on-the-job reliability and increase theft and crime in the ghetto community. The ghetto economy is a system of anarchy that is self-perpetuating.

> This anarchy of the ghetto economy is reflected in the breakdown of its communications. In the normal economy, traditional rules of supply and demand operate efficiently because the existence of a demand effectively communicated to the sources of labor, goods, and capital—and these supplies make their presence felt on the market.[25]

---

[25] Theodore L. Cross, op. cit., p.

The high rate of illiteracy of many of the ghetto residents, including the hard-core unemployed, has created a chaotic economy.

Illiteracy is a major factor in the continuing cycle of frustration in which the ghetto inhabitant finds himself.

The anarchy of the ghetto economy can also be seen in its hardened ability to ignore interest rates. David Caplovitz, the sociologist, in his book, *The Poor Pay More*, pointed out that ghetto residents pay as much as 100 percent annually in interest rates.[26] The Caplovitz study was a major contribution in that it reminded government officials, businessmen, and urbanologists that the poor are consumers. The fact that many ghetto inhabitants cannot obtain credit through normal banking institutions and are, therefore, forced to seek loans from loan sharks at high-interest rates, contributes to their economic frustrations.

The economic anarchy of the ghetto is also visible in the fact that the poor pay higher food prices, higher interest rates, are poor credit risks, and are usually underemployed or unemployed. These conditions serve to keep ghetto residents in a continuing cycle of poverty, and an atmosphere of tension and mistrust is created. All of these factors serve to maintain an economic system that is underdeveloped and is hostile to any efforts to change it.

Any student of business knows that one of the elements of the success of the American entrepreneur has been his ability to plan and predict his cost of supplies, labor, and production. This can be assured in a normal economy

---

[26] David Caplovitz, *The Poor Pay More* (New York: The Free Press, 1963).

because it is stable and reliable. In the ghetto economy, however, labor is totally unpredictable and unreliable.

Credit and capital costs for ghetto projects are not simply excessive; they are completely uncertain and widely variable. Fire and vandalism insurance may not cost more in the ghetto economy; usually it is not available unless the "rioting profile" of a particular city is satisfactory. This unpredictability makes it impossible to establish a reasonably accurate "pro forma" projection of capital costs and operating expenses for projects in the ghettos of our cities.

Role of the Black militants

In 1968, the first effort by a major stock exchange firm to establish a branch in Harlem was undertaken by Shearson, Hammill & Co. This attempt to bring Harlem into the financial mainstream was met by hostility from the Black community. An official of the Congress of Racial Equality charged that the Shearson plan was a conspiracy by government and Wall Street interests to take over Harlem. White Power sees Harlem as the potentially most valuable piece of real estate in New York City. "Harlem is too valuable to remain in Black hands."[27]

It is this type of determination of Black militants to resist any effort of help from the White power structure that will keep the ghetto credit poor.

There is nothing wrong with wanting to have a say in one's destiny or with the concept of community control, but the Black community will not be able to develop a pro-

____

[27] Cross, op. cit., p. 28

ductive economy without the aid of the White business community.

The ghetto residents find themselves in a struggle for survival in a country that possesses great wealth and technical know-how. Studies by the Urban League and O.I.C. have shown that slum dwellers are in a cycle of poverty, yet millions of dollars flow through this ghetto economy every week.

In 1969, a study conducted by the Philadelphia Urban League on the ghettos of North and South Philadelphia showed that millions of dollars were being exchanged for drugs and played on the numbers every day.[28] Recently in Harlem, Black leaders have been trying to get numbers legalized and the profits used to rebuild the community. It has been estimated by community leaders and the police that a million dollars a week passed through the Harlem numbers bank. The numbers business has been highly profitable for many years through most of the slum areas of this country.

In an interview, Charles A. Sterling, an executive with Capital Formation Inc., stated "that traditionally money has been available in the Black community for numbers, big automobiles, and drugs, but until money can be generated in the ghetto for credit and long-range economic programs, the development of a minority enterprise system will not become a reality."[29]

---

[28] Study of the Ghettos of North & South Philadelphia; Philadelphia Urban League, July 1969.

[29] Sterling, Charles A.: Personal Interview, March 10, 1972.

The paradoxical credit system of the ghetto economy can be seen in that it is much easier for a ghetto resident to obtain a loan to buy a Cadillac than it is for him to obtain a loan to go into business.

Another indication of the money that is available in the ghetto community is the number of bars and taverns that are located in these areas. In 1970, the district attorney's office was petitioned by the citizens of the ghetto of North Philadelphia to close down many of the bars in that area. A study by *The Philadelphia Inquirer* showed that in several locations in this area as many as ten bars were found within two blocks of each other.[30] Each of the establishments were doing a prospering business and were owned by absentee owners.

The high "tariff" system of the ghetto prohibits the Black slum resident the luxury of being able to save money, especially enough money to go into business or even buy a house.

The high "tariff" system of the ghetto prohibits the Black ghetto, it does not find its way into the credit channels of the normal economy. It is either used for illegal purposes or because of the high ghetto tariff, just to survive.

The ghetto economy is an ideal situation for loan sharks to operate. This is due to the fact that while they will lend money for higher rates of interest, the money is available. In May 1967, a witness testifying before the Clark Senate Sub-Committee Examination of the War on Poverty stated that a large percentage of new business established by Puerto Rican Americans in New York City was initially financed

---

[30] *The Philadelphia Inquirer*, July 16, 1970, p. 1.

with funds borrowed from loan sharks. In the ghetto community, risk capital is nonexistent. Risk capital is a most vital ingredient for the development of business equities. In the ghetto economy, this is replaced by the high credit costs imposed by loan sharks whose astronomical interest rates and insistence on a short-term maturity prevent the potential ghetto entrepreneur from developing and sustaining a viable commercial enterprise.

Attitude of the Black community

The credit barriers that have been imposed on the Black community have instilled a feeling of total distrust and hostility toward the White power structure. The "tariffs" placed on the slum dweller were a major factor in bringing about the riots of the 1960s in such places as Detroit, Newark, and Watts. After the riots of 1967, the new Detroit Committee of Businessmen negotiated with a militant Black group to create a program of technical assistance to strengthen the Black community. Black moderates viewed this as an attempt to buy off the Black militants. The Black militants, on the other hand, refused to accept the program with the "strings" that the Black moderates had succeeded in having placed on the program. The moderates had agreed to the program only if the administrative controls were provided by the committee. Black militants and some Negro moderates have viewed attempts such as the Poverty Program and the Job Corps as another means of exploiting the Black community because the funds never filter down to the community and the people it was meant to help.

The consensus of the Black community is that the majority of the programs designed to improve the ghetto business community have failed.

Samuel F. Yette, author of *The Choice: The Issue of Black Survival in America*, in chapter two of his book, shows how much of the money intended for the poor and the Black never reach those it was designated to help.[31] Mr. Yette's research shows that the majority of the money intended for the poor was siphoned off by big business or blocked by the red tape of City Hall. It was the latter method used by Mayor Sam Yorty of Los Angeles that helped to bring to a head the tension that ignited the riots in Watts.

In the writer's capacity as the Director of Economic Development and Employment for the Philadelphia Urban League in 1969, there was ample opportunity to observe firsthand the political red tape and exploitation used to deny the poor and Blacks. The author had a chance to see how the technique of tying up funds with red tape in City Hall was used effectively to hinder the Model Cities and Concentrated Employment Programs of Philadelphia. The Black community of Philadelphia was exploited in that programs designed to stimulate jobs and money to improve housing and education never reached the people but was misused for high salaries and software in programs that were not needed.

---

[31] Samuel F. Yette, *The Choice: The Issue of Black Survival in America* (New York: Berkley Medallion Books, 1972), pp. 31–71.

An analysis of the War on Poverty since its inception shows that the Black community has every reason to feel that it has been deceived and exploited. The Kerner Commission in its report on the riots cited the major cause of the riots as poor housing, inadequate health care, and high unemployment. Since publication of the Commission's findings, very little has been done to improve the conditions that caused the riots. The Kerner Commission also described deprivation and Black resentment of White oppression as the long-run causes of the riots. Yet these same conditions are prevalent to a greater degree today. A story in the April 7, 1972, edition of *The New York Times* reported that very little has changed since the Commission gave its recommendations and in some cities, such as Newark, New Jersey, things have gotten worse.[32]

Efforts to create business opportunities in the Black community have usually been exercised in frustration. Black businessmen and White developers who offer assistance in developing projects started have met with disappointment and vandalism. In the May 1, 1972, edition of *The Wall Street Journal,* an article entitled "Black Leaders' Plans to Build Ghetto Stores Often End in Defeat," makes this point very emphatic.[33]

Summary

The ghetto has an economy that abolishes wealth. It keeps the poor and Blacks in a continuous cycle of frustra-

---

[32] *The New York Times*, April 7, 1972, Sec. I, p. 1.
[33] *The Wall Street Journal,* May 1, 1972, Sec. I, p. 1, col. 5.

tion and dependence. While slavery in its cruelest form no longer exists, the White community's need to keep Blacks in a condition of oppression and economic bondage had to be maintained. To accomplish and meet these needs, the ghettos of Watts, South Chicago, North Philadelphia, and Harlem were allowed to develop.

Greed played a major role in the development of slavery in this country and continues to be of major importance in maintaining a system of ghettos. In this country, the very large corporations project an image of concern. They initiate training programs for ghetto workers, and their presidents serve as chairmen of local urban groups. At the same time, Black militants are suspicious of these corporations. Militants ask, "How could the ghetto remain if these men did not permit this to be so?" Like Black Panther and author Eldridge Cleaver, they see General Motors not as a bastion of strength which may be entered but as one which must be destroyed. Cleaver believes corporations know that Black's strength is not in their interest. "While General Motors knows that the unity of these twenty million ragamuffins will spell the death of the system. At all costs, then, they will seek to keep these Blacks from uniting, from becoming bold and revolutionary. These White property owners know that they must keep the Blacks cowardly and intimidated."[34]

The Black man's struggle for survival in the ghetto prohibits him from concentrating his resources on the development of a Black enterprise system.

---

[34] Eldridge Cleaver, *Soul on Ice* (New York: McGraw Hill, 1968), pp. 136–137.

The ghetto economy has amassed such a pernicious array of risks, blocking any effort to introduce credit, that no interest rate is high enough to permit the banker to lend on a basis which is fair to the ghetto borrower and to the owners of the bank.

The fundamental problem in Black business has been its chronic failure to attract, hold, and use institutional credit. Front-end money is essential in starting up a new business.

A tradition-bound economy, such as we find in the ghetto, cannot grow and innovate without developing these discretionary risk funds.

If a minority enterprise system is to become a reality, viable programs to teach ghetto residents how to use credit must be developed. The ghetto must stop being exploited and its residents provided the opportunity of obtaining decent housing, employment, and education.

CHAPTER 4

Case Study of Black Capitalism, The Premium Steak House

The Premium Steak House was first incorporated September 1968, with three persons as sole owners. Each owned a one-third of the business. Their original intent was to establish an eating facility that would remain open for twenty-four hours and provide entertainment for after-hour (2:00 a.m.) patrons over the weekend. Through personally acquired capital, they leased what was once a furniture warehouse and ingeniously renovated the facility into a charming eye-catching building (interior).

Construction soon exhausted their accumulated funds. However, they were able to manipulate and acquire some capital from sources (White) who were noted for lending money to desperate, needy Black entrepreneurs for either astronomical interest rates or the allowance of a jukebox or coin-operated machines to operate on their premises. Subsequently, the renovation was completed approximately five months from its initial start. Apparent eagerness led to a premature opening.

The opening night was sprinkled and flavored with disappointment and difficulties. A lack of adequate wiring caused a short circuit, which darkened the premises while customers were in the midst of eating their dinners. The absence of electricity forced an early departure of the band, and customers fled in anger and dissatisfaction. The poor and inadequate heating system created a chilled and uncomfortable atmosphere for patrons. Several similar experiences eventually forced the business to temporarily shut down for necessary alterations and repairs.

Several weeks thereafter, the steak house was reopened for business. Dissension developed over operating procedures, which later led to dissolvement of the corporation into a partnership (although not officially). Additional financial pitfalls developed, and once again, the business was forced to close temporarily. At this point, a fairly obvious pattern had been established. The steak house was closed more often than it had remained open.

A Small Business Administration loan was sought and obtained through the Minority Business Investment Program sponsored by the Graduate School of Business, Rutgers University, Newark Campus. The amount of the loan was $25,000. The sum total of this allotment was to go toward the total function of all business operating expenditures, i.e., wages, equipment, etc. Contrary to this proposed intent, the partners utilized the funds to expand and immediately opened a discotheque. Ill-planned and ill-conceived, this new venture developed into a disastrous flop both financially and publicity-wise. Constant loitering by teenagers resulted in the closing of the discotheque. Within a few weeks, the steak house closed again; this time, for the purpose of constructing a quick-cook counter which soon proved to be an expensive venture. Sales never reached their expectations and, in fact, dropped to a level far below the average business half its size.

Conclusion

In summary, the reasons for the apparent failure of the Premium Steak House to develop into a viable business enterprise are as follows: The owners formulated plans for a restaurant with limited capital. The plans were ill-conceived and lacked the foresight of possible pitfalls that later developed and overwhelmed them. The owners entered into the venture lacking experience in all areas of business management. Their goal was twofold: to make a quick profit and provide a unique eating facility of a caliber absent from this city (Newark) for Black people. Their dependency and hope upon some miraculous flow of customers and profit never materialized.

Persons who were among the first to patronize the business and often returned, soon ceased to return. They complained bitterly about the inadequate service (cold food, improper equipment), high cost of food, and customers dancing during the consumption of their food. Their failure to correct this situation subsequently "turned off" many customers. Business eventually decreased and cash receipts dipped to such a low point, the management found meeting monthly obligations to be a task of desperation and frustration. What might have been speculated is now fairly evident. Management here was its own worst enemy. In trying to expand before correcting the unwanted ills of the initial facility and improving service and quality of food and equipment, it fell into the pitfalls experienced by so many Black entrepreneurs. Lacking the invaluable knowledge of the basic principles, of accounting practices, expenditures were mismanaged. In addition to these complications, the ability to attract and retain competent and experienced employees doubled the role of the owners who, as a result, had to physically "pitch in" to compensate for the deficiency in personnel. The conglomerate of these ills had not been altered and had produced instead of a viable business a dying investment.

Interviews with officials of the MESBIC (Minority Enterprises Small Business Investment Company) programs provides some interesting facts concerning Black and other Minority small business investors. As revealed by Roy Lee, a Black assistant professor at the Rutgers Graduate School of Business, in a recently written paper containing excerpts from his book, *The Setting for Black Capitalism*, the small business investment idea grew out of a plan devised by the Congress of Racial Equality and presented to President Nixon in 1968. The president promised his support for their community development community plan (CDC). This program called for the return of the profits gained from these corporations to the community to support service projects, such as health care and low-income housing. The community corporations were to be financed by Community Development Banks. These banks were to acquire capital by selling debentures guaranteed by the Federal Government.[35]

The plan never received approval from the Congress but instead was revised by the Nixon administration. Out of this revision, the Office of Minority Business Enterprise was born. It was a coordinating agency with its own administrative funds and the Small Business Administration as its funding agency.

With the establishment of the Executive Order on March 5, 1968, Executive Enterprise was well on its way to becoming a reality. The Small Business Investment Act of 1968 provided the following:

1. Equity and long-term debit investment in small business.
2. $150,000 minimum investment by sponsors of SBICs.
3. Authorization of SBA to purchase guarantee debentures double the amount of private capital investment.
4. SBIC's given special tax privileges.

The minority Business Enterprise Project has since been liquidated, giving "birth to the new concept of Minority Enterprise Small Business Investment Company (MESBIC)." At the Graduate School of Business of Rutgers University, the new MESBIC's program is being sponsored

---

[35] Roy F. Lee, *The Setting for Black Capitalism* (Ithaca, New York, Cornell University Press, In Press).

by ITT for only a management fee large enough to finance one employee. The original Minority Business Enterprise Program was operated and financed by the Graduate School and was funded by MBEP; it ran out of funds. It was sponsored by the Ford Foundation. Under the MBEP, the following facts and figures provide a clear picture of Black and Minority Entrepreneurs Progress.[36]

1. During the latter part of 1970, in Newark, New Jersey, forty-two SBA loans were made to minority entrepreneurs.
2. Most loans were a year old, none less than seven months.
3. Seven were defined as being in trouble
4. Three have definitely failed.
5. Two others have been available for evaluation and are delinquent in payment.

Under the new MESBIC's project, the following facts and figures were provided.[37]

1. Twenty-four loans were awarded.
2. None have existed more than six months.
3. One of twenty-four is considered in desperate trouble and possibly another one.
4. Of the two combined programs, totaling sixty-six loans, 95 percent possessed knowledge of their

---

[36] Interview with Russell C. Mass, Administrative Assistant, Graduate School of Business and Assistant Director of Minority Business Enterprise, May 11, 1971.

[37] Ibid.

business through indirect means (association), 5 percent through direct experience (ownership).

MESBIC's under the directive of the Prudential Insurance Company present somewhat of a contrasting but interesting comparison. Since its inception in April 1970, officials of the MESBIC's Program have interviewed over two hundred prospective clients for loans. More than 50 percent were rejected on the basis of their plans being far out of proportion to guidelines established by MESBIC officials or ill-conceived.[38]

Thus far, Prudential Insurance Company has awarded five loans; it is at present committed to six others. Of the five receiving SBA loans, only two are progressing enough to be considered successful investments. Below is an itemized account of Prudential investments:

Table No. 1

Nature of Business	Amount invested by:	
	Prudential	Bank
1. Electronics Wholesales	$20,000	$100,000
2. Auto Parts Distributor	8,000	30,000
3. Moving and Storage Co.	10,000	-

---

[38] Interview with Stephen A. Tuttle, incumbent President of Prudential Insurance Company's Minority Enterprise Investment Corporation, May 14, 1971.

4. Small Metal Fabricating Factory	8,000	12,000
5. Trucking Co. (Four Trucks)	5,000	25,000

Source: Stephen A. Tuttle, incumbent President of Prudential Minority Enterprise Investment Corporation, expressed the reluctance of Prudential to invest in any business, being fully aware of its propensity toward failure from the outset. "This attitude," he states, "is responsible for the low level of loans we have awarded." Donald McNaughton, President of Prudential, has termed the MESBIC's project successful if one of every ten SBA recipients succeeds. Prudential has met the minimum commitment of $150,000 to the MESBIC's project but, on the other hand, has not raised the additional $150,000 requested by the SBA, although Mr. Tuttle gives assurances that it will.[39]

In the preceding analysis, an opportunity to study a specific case of Black Capitalism, its success and failure, was presented to the reader. These facts and figures are very significant in that they reveal a striking resemblance of progress and hardships experienced by the Premium Steak House and other SBA recipients.

Henry S. Terrell and Andrew I. Brimmer in a paper presented before the Eighty-Second Annual Meeting of the

---

[39] Ibid.

American Economic Association, *The Economic Potential of Black Capitalism* concluded that:

> The ghetto economy, as we understand it today, does not appear to provide profitable opportunity for large scale business investment, and any economic advances made by residents of this marginal sector of economy in all likelihood will not materially alter the investment prospect. This situation is in a large part due to a tendency for affluent Negroes to shop in more diverse national economy... and that...the low income, high level of unemployment, and the poor net financial position of urban Negro families constitutes a poor economic environment for business investment.[40]

In the final analysis to follow, we shall try to answer the question of Black Capitalism and its relevancy to the establishment of the Independent Black University.

If Black Capitalism is failing, how then can it be utilized as a source to support an independent Black university?

---

[40] Andrew F. Brimmer and Henry s. Terrell, *The Economical Potential of Black Capitalism.* A paper presented before the Eighty-Second Annual Meeting of the Association of American Economy, December 29, 1969, Prepared by Andrew F. Brimmer and Henry S. Terrell (New York: New York Hilton Hotel), p. 30

The Black church

The Black church since slavery has had a great influence in the culture, life, and politics of Black people. While other Black financial ventures have defaulted, the Black church has remained fairly stable and financially self-supporting, even during the days of the Depression. The history of this support derives from its membership which, for the most part, are of the lower socioeconomic strata of our society. Few workers in the church are paid for their services such as organist, sexton, minister.

From the establishment of Mother Bethel Church in Philadelphia, Pennsylvania, by Richard Allen in 1786, the Black church has germinated like buds in a garden at the coming of spring. Figures compiled by the 1926 Federal Census of Religious Bodies highlights the growth of the Black church in recent years.

Following 1915, Black congregations built or purchased churches at a rate of 72 percent over fifteen years, an indication that the Black church was a viable business (the church was not viewed by the Black community as a business in 1915).[41] Although at times overburdened with debts resulting from expansion, increased membership as well as by other church or denominational rivalry, the Black church continued to exist through its nickel, dime, and quarter contributions of the membership. Such fund-raising events as gospel shows and contests, cake and pie

---

[41] Benjamin E. Mays and Joseph William Nicholson, *The Black Church* (New York: Russell & Russell Co., 1933), p. 21

sales, and sales of other nature produced considerable sums of money.

These events were and are usually conducted by the "Faithful Few." As one minister states:

> The membership of the church can be divided into three classes. One-third are members in name only. Their names could be dropped from the roll and the church would move unimpaired. The second one-third give and attend on special occasions. The work of the church financially and otherwise is carried on by the last third.[42]

How the Black community views the Black church

And as described in the above statement, the additional financial burden caused by the consistent absence of a third of the membership of the average church is shouldered by the working membership. Miraculously, the church has survived this and other crises. Intergroup rivalry within the church itself has spurred the success of fundraising events when persons and groups outside the church have met with failure. Utilizing every method, from door-to-door soliciting to walking on the street, money, nevertheless continues to find its way into the church's treasury.

In recent years, the Black church has been riddled with criticism regarding its role in the Black community.

---

[42] Ibid., p. 78

Militant Blacks, while challenging the intent and sincerity of the church and its failure to address itself to the problems of the Black community and the "world of what's happening now," have, in spite of all their attempts, failed to secure the loyalty of Black people in general as has the Black church. Few organizations can boast of such loyal support from members of the Black community as can the church.

Notwithstanding the reports and surveys conducted in regard to the Black church, churches have revealed the source of loyalty on which its membership thrives. That the Black church is an independent self-supporting institution is irrefutable. Perhaps its tactics or ability to acquire the ingenuous loyalty and support can be channeled into the establishment of the independent Black university. If the Black university is to remain independent and self-supporting, it must acquire the same undying support enjoyed by the Black church from members of the Black community.

The Black university

The birth of the Black university has been described as one occurring "in adversity, surviving in adversity." Black colleges throughout the country today find themselves facing a crisis for sheer survival.

First conceived in 1867, St. Augustine College of Raleigh, North Carolina, became the first of a long line of Black colleges and universities established for the express purpose of educating the Negro.[43] Over and throughout the years of uncertainty, its staunchest supporter was the Black church. Of the Black colleges existing in 1932, more than 60 percent were supported through contributions made by some Black religious denomination. During a five-year period, one religious denomination contributed $364,300.61 to Wilberforce University in Ohio. However, since the early 1960s, this support of Black universities has diminished considerably.[44]

Unlike the Black church, the Black university has never been a self-supporting institution. Its financial support has been broad and varied. Funds came from federal, state, private, public, and philanthropic foundations.

With the receipt of these contributions as the ultimate source of survival, Black universities find themselves in an obligatory and restricted position regarding policy making. Their educational goal has been one of assimilation of its Black students into the mainstream of White society. Dwindling in students and funds, its future is definitely in question. Part of this crisis can be contributed to the migrant trend of Blacks moving North where the urban communities are offering expanded educational opportunities at lower tuitions.

With the Supreme Court 1954 landmark decision regarding school desegregation,[45] a vast number of Black college students are finding their way into better equipped

---

[43] Dwight Oliver Wendell Holmes, *The Evolution of the Negro College* (New York: Arno Press and the *New York Times*, 1969), p. 186.

[44] Ibid., p. 144.

[45] Supreme Court Decision, *Brown vs. Board of Education*, Washington, D.C., 1954.

White universities, thereby posing a problem for Black universities who now find themselves competing not only with their fellow universities but with the White ones as well. There are many underlying reasons, but one of the obvious ones is the financial grants being offered to Black and other underprivileged minority students.

As Tilden and Wilbert J. LeMelle asserted in their book, *The Black College, a Strategy for Relevancy*:

> The Black college has been no freer than the Afro-American himself has been in seeking effective education. This lack of freedom has been applied equally to both privately and publicly supported institutions. Whatever degree of autonomy these institutions may have enjoyed, they were never at liberty to honestly establish their objectives, much less to faithfully pursue them or confidently expect to achieve them. In this sense, the Black college has been quite similar historically to the institutions of higher learning that were created in several formerly colonized countries that are only now enjoying the measure of freedom required to plan and develop fully without arbitrary and unreal limits imposed upon them.[46]

---

[46] Tilden J. LeMelle and Wilbert J. LeMelle, *The Black College* (New York: Frederic A. Praeger Inc., 1969), p. 7.

In addition to these problems, the Black university finds its educational philosophy and traditional ideological theory being scrutinized and criticized by young Black militant students. Competent teachers are difficult to obtain, and the future seems even bleaker; and unless the administrators of Black Universities devise some innovative means to compete with the crisis at hand and weather the storm, Black universities as we know them will perish.

Conclusion

Amidst this era of protest, numerous White institutions of higher education find themselves under attack from all fronts. White students are protesting environmental pollution, the War in Indochina, social injustice, etc. Black students on the other flank have centered their protests on the establishment of relevant education, namely, Black Studies. Originating in the late 1960s at San Francisco State College and radiating across the country with the force of an uncontrolled storm, many major White universities possessing a sizable number of Black students were hit with demands for Black Studies.

More than two years have transpired and many Black students in White universities find themselves with only token programs of Black studies. While overt protests by Black students have subsided, the underlying resentment, disenchantment, and struggle continue. Thus the question is raised: If White universities are unyielding in intent to refuse Black students an education that is beneficial to their culture, political, social, and economical life in the mainstream of American society, why then attend such a school? Why not attend a Black university? As we noted in the previous section, such a trend offers little in terms of meaningful education, as the Black universities are perpetuating the same educational philosophy and ideology Black students seek to escape.

The question of a relevant education is an important one. True, culture identification is important, but Black students must ask themselves if Black studies will provide the knowledge and business training necessary to achieve success in the business community.

The more important issue is that the Black student obtain the proper orientation in the areas of accounting, business philosophy, management, marketing, finance, and other business disciplines. If Blacks are to make any progress in the business field, this should be their objective.

Goals of the Black institution

The goal of the institution of higher learning as we now know it to be is to assimilate its students into the mainstream of American society. While not possessing a financial independent status, Black universities find themselves virtually in the same position as White financed Black studies in White universities. "One cannot bite the hand that feeds it" without suffering in some respect. And in this respect, financial death is the result for many Black universities who must rely heavily upon support from the government, both state and federal, who can sever their accreditation and financial subsidies, as well as other White philanthropic foundations. The need, therefore, for the establishment of an all-Black, independent, self-supporting institution of higher learning becomes eminent. How can we genuinely achieve this goal with lasting results? We can first begin by developing an undying loyalty and devotion for this idea, such as that found in the Black churches. We can create a sense of nationalism in the fashion of Marcus Garvey, founder of the United Negro Improvement Association, which in the early 1920s, reflected the attitude of many Blacks who rejected assimilation in the White society as "impossible to achieve and a form of self-geno-cide."[47] Hopefully, with this attitude, spiritually, philosophically, and ideologically, we can revert to the "days of yesterday" when the church contributed inspiringly toward Black education. One must also evaluate other means of lasting financial support. In the case study of Black capitalism, the selfish and avaricious aims of the Black entrepreneurs was noted. What was particularly stressed was their naivete toward the capitalist system which they attempted to function in, which resulted in failure.

As a result of a long history of neglect by the Black community and Black universities, Black business cannot be counted upon to immediately respond or rush to support this university concept.

The reduction of the number of Black universities into one enormous educational complex is a viable concept, but unless it is independent and self-supporting, it will experience the same pitfalls that most Black colleges and universities are today experiencing.

---

[47] LeMelle and LeMelle, op. cit., p. 7.

The Muslims under the leadership of the Hon. Elijah Muhammad have organized one of the few nationalist-minded organizations; they have utilized Black capitalism to finance many of their ventures, namely the University of Islam in Chicago, the only true independent Black university existing in America. However, "few people" such as Debby Brown, daughter of Ray Brown, renowned defense lawyer and lecturer noted, "will support such a radical concept." If these attitudes are prevalent among most Blacks, then the need to find a means to financially support this concept is enhanced. Contrary to most reports and surveys describing the Black community as being unable to…"provide profitable opportunity for large-scale business investment." There is money in the Black community. The numbers racket flourishes and millions of dollars are spent over a three-day weekend in bars and night clubs across the nation. Black people are the most consistent purchasers of fashionable apparel. Obviously, these illustrations could provide profitable resources which could be utilized in the financing of the university.

One cannot afford to frown upon these suggestions but rather must evaluate them for their worthwhileness while disregarding the moral "hang-ups" and recognizing such as a way of life. Until an independent self-supporting Black university has been developed, this will remain merely a lifeless concept.

CHAPTER 5

The Role of Corporate America in the Development of Black Capitalism

In 1968, just before Richard M. Nixon was inaugurated president, his counselor, Daniel P. Moynihan, gave him a "Memorandum for the President on the Position of Negroes."[48] The memorandum offered the president the following advice: "The Negro lower class must be dissolved by transforming it into a stable working class population. It is the low-income marginally employed, poorly educated, disorganized slum-dwellers" whom "Black extremists use to threaten White society with the prospects of mass arson and pillage." Therefore, said Moynihan, these people must be developed into a viable working class—people with dignity, purpose, and provided the opportunity to make a good living.

During the 1968 presidential campaign, candidate Richard Nixon spoke about Black capitalism as a means

---

[48] "69 Moynihan Memo to President Urged Jobs for Negroes," *The New York Times*, March 1, 1970, p. 1.

of giving ghetto residents "a piece of the action." His suggestions, certainly consistent with the Moynihan strategy, were met with favor by important elements in big business and the Black community. Business saw both financial and public relations value in the plan. Blacks sensed that if given the incentive of potential profit, business could make a substantial impact on ghetto growth.

In this chapter, the role industry has played in the development of Black capitalism will be examined and discussed, as well as the role that corporate America must play if the theme "Black Capitalism" is to become a reality and not just a slogan.

Black community's view of corporate America

The Black community's expectations of the role that major corporations would play in the eradication of poverty and unemployment was very high in the election year of 1968. To put into proper perspective why the masses of Blacks were so hopeful that industry could save America, one has to understand that the free enterprise system has made America what it is today—the richest country in the world. It should also be noted that the Nixon administration is not solely to blame for the failure of Black business. Blacks must share the blame in the failure and realize that Black capitalism will not become a reality without some changes in developing the concept.

The Black community must understand that the development of a minority enterprise system will not happen quickly. Blacks must also understand that they have a role to play if the corporations are to provide assistance to minority business development.

Why does the Black community mistrust big business?

This is a very valid and important question that must be answered.

In the 1960s, under the John F. Kennedy and Lyndon B. Johnson administrations, the War on Poverty was initiated. Big business was to play a major role in providing training and the "software" equipment to make the Black poor more employable. The Job Corps Centers under the OEO programs were mostly contracted to major corporations such as IBM, RCA, and ITT. The only Black organization to receive a contract to operate a Job Corps Center was Alpha Kappa Alpha sorority, a social organization of Black college women.

"Corporations received large amounts of money to run these training centers, which were mostly attended by Black youth from the ghetto. The money that was intended to aid the poor and Blacks ended up in the coffers of these corporations as profits."[49] The philosophy of these centers was to provide remedial training and not to make the trainee employable. It soon became evident to civic and government leaders that more money was spent to purchase materials and software than was used for actual development of the Job Corps trainees' skills. This resulted in the closing of several of the larger centers run by corporations, such as the Camp Kilmer Center run by RCA.

---

[49] Samuel F. Yette, The Choice: *The Issue of Black Survival in America*, (New York: Berkley Medallion Books, 1972), p. 132

It also increased the distrust of the Black community toward the motivation of big corporations.

This attitude of mistrust also stemmed from the belief by militants and extremists that the ghetto could not exist without the insensitivity of the entire White community, particularly the business community.

There is some validity to this assumption. Major corporations have practiced discrimination for years and only recently have they made any attempts to provide employment opportunities for all races. When one looks at the personnel of major corporations, one sees very few Blacks in positions of responsibility. Most Blacks in corporate positions are in what the author calls pseudo-executive positions. Blacks have usually been placed in "show" jobs and have not been given adequate advancement opportunities. These practices have not endeared big business to the Black community, especially young Blacks on campuses today.

Corporate America has not used its position of power to aid the Black and poor in their efforts to be included in the economic mainstream of this country. The fact is that corporations have not used their economic leverage to bring about open housing, to improve local school systems, and eliminate the ghetto conditions. This lack of commitment on the part of industry reinforces the militants' mistrust of the desire of business to aid the ghetto residents of America.

In the previous chapters, it was pointed out that one of the major problems facing the Black entrepreneur was the lack of credit and money services. This fact has aided the Black market money supplier and gorging credit merchants.

Black militants preach that the large metropolitan banks are financing the slumlords, gorging credit merchants and the loan sharks.

The banks have not successfully refuted these charges. The result has been increased hostility of many Blacks toward the banking industry. This is illustrated by the organized efforts now being carried out to encourage mass voluntary bankruptcies as a means of punishing local merchants, banks, and finance companies. Meetings of Black militants teach the advantages and techniques of bankruptcy.

Black militants have used boycotts to show their displeasure at being exploited by corporations of other industries. Rev. Leon Sullivan, founder and chairman of the Opportunities Industrialization Centers of America Inc., led a group of four hundred ministers to boycott the Tastykake Company of Philadelphia because of their discriminatory hiring practices.

The extremist element of the Black community may not be completely accurate in their charges against business but industry has put itself in the position where it can be accused and cannot answer their accusers.

Since the riots of the 1960s, corporate America has made an effort to eradicate the causes of the hostility in the ghetto community. Business has made an effort to recruit Blacks and other minorities for executive and middle management positions. The Black community views this effort as being forced upon business by the law. Many in the Black community and Black leaders feel that industry is providing only lip service.

William H. Brown III, Chairman of the Equal Employment Opportunity Commission, states: "There is more racial animosity in America today than ever before." This animosity is being exemplified by both White and Black. Mr. Brown also states that business doesn't believe equal employment is good business.[50]

LaMonte Owens, President of LaMonte Owens Associates, a minority recruiting consulting firm, states that many companies are not sincere in their efforts to hire qualified Blacks. He also feels that Black college students have become disillusioned with the rhetoric of companies claiming to be an equal opportunity employer.[51]

Today most business corporations are loudly proclaiming, with great smugness and self-satisfaction, that they are equal opportunity employers and that they do not tolerate discrimination against Black men and women in such matters as recruiting, hiring, promoting, compensating, and determining the terms and conditions of employment. The offices of most corporations are liberally plastered with such high-sounding statements of corporate policy. Companies have spent enormous sums of money advertising nationally that they are making great progress in utilizing Black managerial talent and of the tremendous opportunities for Black managers and executives in their companies.

The truth is this is not the case, as William H. Brown III, EEOC Chairman, has found in the term he has

---

[50] William H. Brown III, "The EEOC's Chairman Comments on the Persistence of Racism," *MBA Journal*, Vol. 6, No. 4, January 1972.

[51] Statement by LaMonte Owens, personal interview, January 12, 1972.

been in charge of the Equal Employment Opportunity Commission.

Marshall Monroe, Placement Counselor with Richard Clarke Associates, minority consultants, says that "business was sincere for a short time, but in the last year or so, they are just playing games."[52]

The Black communities are tired of promises; they want to see companies provide meaningful opportunities for Blacks and other minorities.

When one examines the situation of the Black man in efforts for equal job opportunity, the only thing that has changed is that the door to business has been cracked open a little.

Clarence M. Dunnaville Jr., an attorney for Western Electric Company, supports this contention. He states:

> All that has really changed in the past few years is that corporations have shifted the point at which they begin to apply discriminatory practices against their Black management employees. Rather than excluding Blacks altogether from the ranks of management, the current practice by the overwhelming majority of corporate employers is to prevent the aspiring Black manager from advancing beyond the first or second level of supervision.[53]

---

[52] Marshall Monroe, Personal Interview, March 2, 1972.

[53] Clarence M. Dunnaville Jr. and others, "Black Executives: The Darkies at the Bottom of the Stairs," *MBA Journal*, Vol. III, No. 7, April–May 1969.

Black militants point to these conditions facing Blacks who strive for the executive suite and feel justified in accusing industry of continuing its racist practices.

The Black community must not get caught up in the trap of playing accuser; it must offer alternatives and programs that will aid the development of Black managers and executives.

Corporate America must reexamine its practices and immediately seek ways to eradicate the hostile attitude that the Black community feels toward its members.

If America is to eliminate the ghettos and if Blacks are to share in the tradition of free enterprise, big business must be willing to share its knowledge and provide opportunities to obtain responsible positions for all minorities who are willing to work and earn them.

What the White power structure can do

Man is living in an age of crisis and tension. The individual citizen and the corporate citizen are living in a time when man is concerned about his very survival. There is the concern of pollution, inflation, and the racial crisis. Today, the corporation is coming under attack for its performance. A frequent charge is that, through their performance, corporations are making our communities dirtier, more polluted, and less congenial. Another charge states that corporations are too heavily oriented toward profits at the expense of service to the community. Corporations are also being criticized on the basis that their performance is too often flawed because minorities don't participate equally.

The question has been raised as to whether corporations have a social responsibility. MIT professor, Paul A. Samuelson, a 1970 Nobel Prize winner for his economic theories and writings, believes that they do. He states, "A large corporation these days not only may engage in social responsibility; it had damn well better try to do so."[54]

The ghetto presents many problems for the residents that live there, but its major problem is unemployment. The high rate of unemployment is the catalyst for all the other problems and frustrations found in the ghetto.

America must, if it is to solve the employment problems of the poor, provide new jobs in our ghetto areas. America must create an economic climate in which business, especially those owned and managed by members of minority groups and residents of ghetto areas, will be willing to establish new facilities and expand existing facilities in the centers of our urban and rural poverty areas.

It must be recognized that the role of private enterprise can only complement other community efforts, and business must be willing to lead and provide management, counseling, and financial assistance. Private corporations are, of course, responsible to their stockholders. Largescale investment in poverty areas will certainly be more costly and difficult than investment elsewhere. Land, transportation, training of workers, extra supervision—all these are so costly in ghetto areas as to make investment there, under

---

[54] Samuel Feinberg, "Profit, Social Conscience Compatible," *Women's Wear Daily*, Tuesday, January 5, 1971, p. 1.

present conditions, uneconomical. If private business is to provide assistance, it must be provided various financial incentives and motivated for its own survival.

The government, in its efforts to attract the aid of private enterprise, has enacted bills such as the Manpower Development and Training Act and the Economic Opportunity Act. Despite these efforts, the plight of the Black and poor has not improved.[55] A recent survey, conducted by the *New York Times* and reported in the April 7, 1972 edition supports this contention.

In 1969, the National Advisory Commission on Civil Disorders recommended that business be given tax incentives as an inducement to start business in the nation's ghetto areas.[56] Tax incentives and other financial inducements are very important, but they alone cannot solve the problem.

A capital creation program is clearly needed. Provisions must be made for a mechanism which will break the cycle that turns capital away from business seeking to establish facilities in ghetto areas. In short, a flow of short-term and long-term loans must be provided to those businesses which will open and expand badly needed industrial and commercial facilities and help turn those economically deprived into areas of hope and opportunity.

Capital, while vital, is not enough to establish viable businesses owned and managed by members of minority groups and low- and moderate-income residents of poverty

---

[55] Fredrick D. Sturdivant, *The Ghetto Market Place* (New York: The Free Press, 1969), p. 194.

[56] Ibid., p. 199.

areas. These groups have been excluded so long from business activities that they also need technical management assistance.

Minority and poverty area citizens must know when and how to get assistance, both from government and private industry. They must be able to understand and put together complicated financial arrangements and be able to communicate with other businessmen.

Business has the experts and technical know-how to provide the talent to assist in the development of a minority enterprise system.

A program for business

Any business programs designed to aid the ghetto should include at least the following:

They should include members of minority groups and ghetto residents to motivate them to enter business or to expand existing businesses.

They should motivate and encourage minority members to take special courses in business, major in business at the undergraduate level, and establish scholarship and assistance programs for MBA and undergraduate students. Young Blacks today do not want to be given a job to fail. What they want is a chance to learn and develop skills that will aid them in business.

The University of Pennsylvania's Wharton School of Business is involved in such a program to provide business training for disadvantaged minority youth. The program was started as a result of meetings with the Wharton faculty and leaders of the Black community in Philadelphia. This program, called the Community Wharton Educational Program, has proven to be very successful since its inception. Today, there are over 120 students from the program in regular college business programs, and they have improved their employment situation as a result of their training in this program.

Dr. Robert Nason, professor of marketing, University of Pennsylvania, states:

> Business courses are essential to the development of a minority business enterprise. We have proven that when educational institutions, community groups, and business work together, the job can get done. We would like to see more cooperation from the business community.[57]

Private enterprise must improve its record of hiring minorities at *all levels* of the corporate structure. One must honestly examine the employment picture of Blacks and other minorities to gain a better understanding of the deficiencies in the minority business community.

Corporations must stop playing the game of lip service and hire minorities into their management and development programs and provide the same upward mobility opportunities that have long been afforded Whites.

Blacks who are interested must be given the chance to learn how the financial, marketing, and procurement

---

[57] Robert Nason, PhD., Personal Interview, Feb. 4, 1972.

functions of business operate. Industry must be willing to develop Blacks and prepare them for supervisory and management positions. Blacks must be encouraged by high school and college counselors to major in business and business must be willing to select Blacks for these positions.

Business must be willing to establish communication with the Black institutions of higher learning. Executives and managers from the corporate community must be encouraged to serve as advisors and provide input to these colleges to help them upgrade their business curricula. Major corporations *must* be willing to hire Black college professors during the summer months, so they can get first-hand experience of the changes taking place in industry. The quality of education in most Black schools is not equal to that of their White counterparts. Business can eliminate this inequality by providing managerial and financial assistance to these institutions.

Industry must use its economic leverage to bring about open housing, which aids in bringing about better educational opportunities for minorities who can afford to move into a better-class neighborhood.

Once the program of hiring and upgrading Blacks and other minorities is moving and has begun to have some effect on the color scheme of management, the business community should begin the next step.

Step two of a program to assist the development of a minority business enterprise system should be the creation of new business opportunities. Major corporations in urban areas should be motivated to forming committees committed to providing subcontracts, thus helping minority businessmen obtain contracts from the federal and local governments.

The business community must also be willing to lend its staffs to serve as consultants to minority businessmen to teach them how to develop and negotiate lines of credit and establish accounting procedures and cost-control techniques. The White business community *must be* willing to impart its knowledge and skills if a minority enterprise system is to become a part of the American free enterprise system.

Business and community groups working together can develop this kind of program. As Richard Kennard, President of Capital Formation, states: "A partnership of business and the minority community can develop meaningful programs that will have some impact on the minority community."[58]

A partnership that failed

In 1968, militant Blacks were surprised to hear Richard M. Nixon speak strongly in favor of a Black capitalism program. Nixon thought that property rights had to precede human rights. He believed that ownership provides economic power, and the latter is the basis for independence and security. The leaders of the Congress of Racial Equality (CORE) sought and received Nixon's support for an economic plan on which they were working.

The plan CORE developed called for the creation of community development corporations, each of which in

---

[58] Richard c. Kennard, Personal Interview, March 11, 1972.

turn would generate a series of business establishments. The profits from these businesses would be put back into the community by supporting service projects such as health care and low-income housing. The community corporations were to be financed by community development banks. The banks were to acquire capital by selling debentures guaranteed by the federal government. This concept has been tried in the past by the White community, and it proved to be a failure then also.

The plan had many weaknesses; the major one was the limiting of "outside" investors in the areas defined by the boundaries of each community development corporation. Any business not owned by community residents was to operate only on a "turkey" basis with the understanding that it be sold to the Community Development Corporation once it became profitable. Tax incentives were limited to those of the Community Development Corporation subsidiaries and government funds could not be secured unless the community development bank had turned down a loan.

Under this plan, the entrepreneur would have little opportunity for independent action. This plan failed for two reasons: First, it represented an attempt by community capitalism to control individual or entrepreneurial capitalism that existed in the communities surrounding the Community Development Corporation's areas. Secondly, it failed because it was just another form of oppression and it excluded making use of the know-how of the business community. It was foolish to expect the White corporate structure to help out on a charitable basis.

The MESBIC as a tool

Private enterprise has a history of excellent performance when compared to other forms of enterprise. Their basis for survival is their own ingenuity and hard work. Profit, to the businessman, is the ultimate criterion of success. This is not so with government or nonprofit organizations.

The Nixon Plan for "Black capitalism" was basically sound because it took this into account. It provided for a business-oriented organization whereas the Congress of Racial Equality Plan was too much community oriented. In both plans, the community played a major role, although somewhat less in the Nixon Plan. The Nixon Plan provides for greater expertise input than does the other plan, and this is a very important factor. The lack of managerial and executive expertise is a major problem in ghetto areas, and the way in which this expertise was designed in the CORE plan was difficult to translate to a practical method.

The Nixon Plan included an Office of Minority Business Enterprise (OMBE) established by executive order on March 5, 1969. The Office of Minority Business Enterprise was located in the Commerce Department and was responsible for the coordination of all federal programs which are designed to assist minority persons seeking to establish or expand businesses. It also had the responsibility to encourage and assist the efforts of the private sector, state, and local governments and coordinate them with federal efforts; establish a national clearinghouse for information on minority enterprise: and establish an advising council of outstanding private citizens.

Thus the role of OMBE is purely a coordinative one with only administrative funding responsibility. The Small Business Administration is the funding agent.

The Office of Minority Business Enterprise gave birth to the concept of Minority Enterprise Small Business Investment Company (MESBIC).

The Minority Small Business Investment Companies are directed solely at minorities and were given special tax incentives allowing for ordinary loss deduction rather than capital loss deduction. They were also allowed 100 percent deduction on dividends received from investments for domestic corporations. They were initiated to provide for established corporations to make equity and long-term debts investments in small business concerns owned or started by minorities.

Mr. George R. Glass, President of the General Foods sponsored MESBIC, states: "To minority businessmen, the MESBICs offer a direct localized source of venture capital and long-term credit and access to sophisticated managerial assistance and markets. The combination of funds and managerial assistance offers the best assurance for success."[59] This is very important as it would provide a vital ingredient to eradicate the major weaknesses facing Black businessmen.

White banks have always been hesitant to lend to minorities; this is true even though the government guarantees 90 percent of their loans. This is the weakest link in the MESBIC plan. Another weak point in the plan is the size of the investment made by the sponsor corporations.

---

[59] George R. Glass, Personal Interview, March 8, 1972.

The minimum investment is $150,000 but the OMBE officials are aware that this is far from being sufficient to support a successful venture. They feel that a more accurate figure would be about $300,000.

Another weakness of the MESBIC approach seems to be aimed at only helping the "little guy" and that they have no intention of making anyone rich. The emphasis ought not to be on who gets rich, but the goal should be to develop minority business. The emphasis ought not to be on who gets rich, but to develop programs to assist minorities to achieve full participation in this country's free enterprise system.

The private sector consists of small, medium-sized, and very large businesses.

Mr. William Haskins, Senior Consultant with Arthur D. Little Inc. and former Urban League Consultant to the National Alliance of Business, states:

> The MESBIC program is now entering its second phase: that involving business leaders to provide the managerial skills and technical know-how. What we should be addressing ourselves to is not developing minority business but also developing more Blacks to enter the field of business via school, corporations, or entrepreneurial routes.[60]

---

[60] William Haskins, Personal Interview, April 9, 1972.

Summary

The Minority Business Investment Corporation is a step in the right direction, but it will not provide the solution to this major problem. What is needed is commitment from government and business. This alone, however, will not be enough to secure the success of the program.

There must be certain changes in the MESBIC concept, such as increasing the minimum investment of sponsor corporations.

The Small Business Administration should guarantee 100 percent of funds loaned to clients of the MESBICs by the banks. MESBICs should be managed by a management team of minority group members for a fee and equity participation based on their success.

Corporations should be willing to lend the minorities working for them to MESBICs trying to get started. If they don't have trained minority group members available, they should contact business schools and hire and train minority graduates for some of their positions.

The Black community must be willing to prepare more of its members to seek positions in the industry. They must encourage young Blacks to enter business programs at the undergraduate and graduate levels.

Business and the Black community must understand that business will not assist minority business development for charitable reasons. They must do it for its own self-interest.

America has the technical know-how to solve its problems for twenty-two million impoverished Americans. Not to do so will be to endanger the free enterprise system.

CHAPTER 6

Summary and Conclusions

When one studies the history of the Black man's role in American business, one soon discovers that the status of Black business has declined. Instead of growing and developing from generation to generation, Black business has stagnated in a cycle of frustration.

Black Americans have suffered because they have been denied the right to participate in the economic mainstream, and their confidence in their own ability to learn and develop their business skills has been impeded by prejudice.

The effect of racism has left a terrible mark on the Black man, as well as the White; it has divided the nation and created an atmosphere of mistrust and hatred that must be overcome if this country is to survive economically and socially.

It was Calvin Coolidge who said, "The business of America is business." This is no mere philosophical generalization. Any student of American history knows the relationship between business and the Federal Government has always been an intimate one. One does not have to look to recent Federal legislation; all that is required is a casual study of the nation's economic history.

It has only been recently that the Federal Government has shown active concern with small business and even more recently with minority business.

The changes that have taken place in society and business over the years make it increasingly difficult for smaller businesses to survive. This is a fact that has hurt the Black man in his struggle to succeed in business.

Method of research

The major portion of the methodological approach to this paper centered around the use of the books, papers, periodicals, and other professional literature presently available dealing with the subject of Black capitalism. This information has been coupled with interviews with Black businessmen, civil rights workers, Black entrepreneurs, Blacks working in the field of economic development, and the author's firsthand experiences in the field of economic development.

The findings

While much has been expected of Black capitalism, an evaluation of the subject reveals that little has been delivered. Despite the plethora of government agencies, private enterprise, and community organizations engaged in developing a viable system of "Black capitalism, capital assets acquired by Black entrepreneurs and businessmen over the past two years amounted to only 0.005 percent of United States industry's capital expenditures in the same period."[61]

In researching this paper, several factors considered barriers to the development of Black capitalism were disproved as being major obstacles to the formation of new Black businesses. While there have been some efforts of Black economic development, there have been failures. Most efforts have been dedicated to achievement.

Most often given as the causes of failure are the following four factors that in researching on this paper proved to be excuses: lack of capital, lack of Black entrepreneurs, lack of business competence of Black people, and hostility of the Black community and its leaders to proposed economic programs.

Lack of capital

A deficiency of capital is almost always mentioned as the most significant obstacle seen by would-be entrepreneur, Black or White, in the way of his turning his idea into a successful business venture. It is certainly true that the Black people have not had access to capital and credit to the degree that the White man has, nor do they have personal capital, such as savings, securities, and other financial investments which they can invest in a business venture.

It was this barrier that prompted the first efforts by governmental agencies, businesses, and civil rights organizations to develop programs that would provide greater

---

[61] Interview with Samuel Beard, President of the Development Council. May 6, 1972.

access to capital, thus encouraging Black entrepreneurship. Capital is not a dynamic force. It is seldom, if ever, even catalytic.

Money has always been available for good sound ideas that have been researched and projected to be successful. An example of this is the oversubscription of many new public stock offerings by investors. Since a Small Business Administration Loan is exempt from calculations of reserve requirements, it can be used to secure Federal Reserve Accounts; thus commercial banks can recoup their money from the Federal Reserve banks, and this makes it attractive in a tight money market.

The lack of capital theory has been cited as a major deterrent to the development of new Black businesses. While this is a problem, the findings show that in many cases, it is unsound business ideas that are the real barrier: the Black community cannot expect business to provide capital for business ideas that have proven to be unsuccessful in the past o that are obsolete.

Lack of Black entrepreneurs

The lack of Black businessmen is not a real obstacle while it is true that in the Black community one cannot find the wealth of business managers, engineers, and scientists needed to develop new businesses to the degree that they are available in the White community; there are Blacks capable of succeeding in the business world. The Black community produce men capable of starting businesses. It is only an excuse on the part of both the White and Black communities.

Entrepreneurship is a blend of a man's personality traits, his independence, venturesomeness, ambition, and determination. While their opportunities have been limited, Blacks with these characteristics have started business ventures. Men such as Henry G. Parks of Parks Sausages, John H. Johnson of *Ebony*, George Johnson of Johnson Products, and the Black-owned Summit Laboratories, a cosmetic firm in Indianapolis, are a few examples that Blacks with sound ideas can make it in business.

Many Blacks who have not had the opportunity to use their skills in legal enterprises have developed their entrepreneurial skills in illegal activities or in religious activities. The Black minister and Black hustler are both entrepreneurs.

The most successful Black capitalism efforts in the country were founded by the Rev. Leon Sullivan of Philadelphia. His Opportunities Industrialization Centers are considered by many in private business and the government to be the best of government private Black programs.

Lack of business competence

The lack in business know-how and training is often given as the reason for failure of some new Black businesses and the reason why many are unable to find financing. The lack of formal education and the lack of business experience are more typical of the Black community than the White community. It is also true that there is an absence of a cultural orientation toward business in the Black community. True, these conditions do exist. They are not the cause for failure; they are excuses. More intensified management training may be required, but the success of other ethnic group entrepreneurs without cultural or educational business training indicates that this is not a major barrier.

Educators have proven that people learn what is necessary to learn at the time they need to learn it. The army has demonstrated that men can learn those skills necessary to do whatever job has to be done. The theory about management training is the result of an unwillingness to accept the normal new-venture failure rate because of the social implications.

Sometimes, this lack of competence is not incompetence at all. It is a form of rejection. Potential Black entrepreneurs understand business principles perfectly but want no part of Whites. This becomes a serious problem when Blacks insist that they control the business, although they have not put up any or only a minor share of the equity capital, or that the community, not the financial backer or the entrepreneur, be the primary beneficiary of the business. Control of a business for a minor share of equity is also a hang-up with White businessmen, but it is almost universal with Black businessmen because of social and economic suppression.

Hostility of the Black community and its leaders

Apathy or outright hostility of Blacks toward programs designed to assist them through Black capitalism projects, employment, and economic development projects have also been cited as major obstacles. At first glance, the statistics seem to support this observation. When we examine closely the programs designed to assist Blacks in the development of business and job skills, it becomes apparent that most of the programs are obsolete. Turnover statistics among unskilled trainees in both Black and White companies have been frustrating and paradoxical considering the increased demands of Blacks for jobs. Theodore Cross in his book, *Black Capitalism*, states that the usual reason given for this hostility is that Blacks believe that many of the programs to provide help are just another form of exploitation. This may be true of some of the efforts to help Blacks, but there have been programs that have made an impact. An example of a sound viable program is in the Capital Formation Inc., bank depository program. This theory is also supported because, despite past surveys and experiences that show that Blacks will not support (as laborers or customers) a Black business just because it is Black, this is frequently given as one of the major reasons to start a business that is doomed from the start.

Blacks have been accused of being too lazy to learn business skills because they have not supported those training programs designed to train Blacks for employment in business and industry. The truth is that most of these programs trained people for dead-end positions. Blacks and other minorities might be poor, but they are not stupid. This type of training has produced a new form of welfare, with individuals going from one dead-end training program to another. The Black community's harsh attitude is not a result of the racial prejudice that has been directed its way but stems from the frustration of being trained for dead-end jobs that will not provide future opportunity or upward mobility.

The argument that the Black community is apathetic and hostile is not a real one; it is used as subterfuge to divert the White community from examining the real causes for failure of the Black capitalism programs.

Blacks had been promised that the program of Black capitalism would help them escape the ghetto and its life of poverty. They were led to believe by the public relations efforts of the Johnson and Nixon administrations this would occur overnight. The Black community was not given the hard cold facts that the problems of the poor and unskilled cannot be solved in a short time.

Blacks, on the other hand, now realize that they cannot rely on someone else to build a viable community for them; Blacks must help themselves. Blacks also have seen, as the research findings show, that they have been exploited by Blacks as much as they have been misled by Whites.

The Black community and its leaders are not hostile to the programs designed to aid Black capitalism and employment; they are just tired of being given the same poor quality of jobs and training with different window dressing.

The promises of a better future and a piece of the action gave rise to their hopes, but the performance of the government, business, and the White and Black communities has created a feeling of frustration and despair.

Conclusion

The program of Black capitalism should be reviewed, and changes need to take place in the philosophy of the program.

The title "Black Capitalism" should be the first thing that is reviewed. Black Capitalism is a derogatory term that implies incompetence. The term Black Capitalism is another way of stating that Blacks are not capable of participating in the free enterprise on the same level as the White businessman. It is another form of segregation; it is similar to establishing a dual system of education, only in this case it is having two levels of business operating at one time.

In researching this paper, I reached the conclusion that rhetoric of Black capitalism needs to be de-escalated and that it is the wrong approach in solving the problems of brining Blacks into the economic mainstream.

What would be more appropriate is to address ourselves to how we can bring more Blacks and minorities into the business arena. The creation of a Black Capitalism system should not be our primary goal. What should be our goal is the development of the young Black's skills via education, training, and business opportunities.

The findings of this chapter also made it clear that one of the major barriers to the development of the Black

Capitalism program is that we have been asking business and the government for the wrong kind of assistance.

Business development

The Black community must take the initiative in developing programs to motivate their young people in the elementary school toward business. Blacks will have to encourage their junior and senior high school youngsters to ask about the opportunities in business from their school counselors.

The Black community must make every effort to seek to improve the opportunities of their youngsters to enroll in business programs and courses at the undergraduate and graduate levels in college.

It must be emphasized that taking this route to develop business skills in the Black community will take longer, but it will increase the chance of success for future generations of Blacks in business.

Business must take a major role in this type of plan to bring about an increase in the number of Blacks in business. They can do this by making an all-out sincere effort to develop Blacks through their management training programs; also by assisting Black colleges to improve their business curriculum by meeting the school department heads to discuss what business looks for in their applicants and the kinds of courses that are needed to produce a qualified individual in today's business world.

Although there are many cases where business has not made a concerted effort to assist in the development of the minority community business skills, it cannot be held completely at fault. Business has been asked to provide financial backing and to release control of new business that they participate in with Blacks and to provide just plain charity. This is wrong. The Black community cannot and should not ask the White business community for charity.

The objective of the Black business community should be to get business to serve in a partnership with the Black community to develop the business skills of Blacks because it would be in its own self-interest.

If business is asked to share in the potential profits and not asked just to develop business opportunities and also to provide a solution for the social ills of the community, there would be better cooperation.

Experience has shown that it is difficult enough to start a new business and survive, without at the same time trying to cure the social problems, such as health care and housing.

The Federal Government has been asked to provide more than it can give. The guaranteed loans, contracts, technical assistance grants, tax incentive and market studies, and all other supportive programs that federal agencies have been asked to administer cannot create viable businesses.

Programs are designed to be incentives, but too often the constraints of politics prohibits rather than encourages the development of the entrepreneurs essential for a viable Black capitalism program. These constraints prohibit proposals for programs from developing into business ventures. Another factor that works against the agencies involved is the fact that many of the people involved are motivated by politics instead of concern.

The truth is, if the government were able, society could not afford the cost on a pay-as-you-go basis to recruit the necessary personnel to put together all the creative elements of a new venture.

The government, in an effort to overcome the fact that it would be impossible to hire the people needed to develop the necessary programs, has relied on volunteers from private business, the government, and the community. Although enlisting volunteers has negated this problem, it has created another problem. The volunteers' attitude toward the programs they were aiding and the people they were trying to help overshadows the help they render. Too often the volunteers' attitude is one of putting down the ghetto residents they are trying to help.

These men and women, because they are volunteering time and in some cases financial assistance, make the mistake of looking upon their work as charitable or social contributions. They disregard the business principles that made their business successful. To make allowances for Blacks, by not seeking a reasonable return on their investment, is degrading to the Black people they are trying to help. What becomes quite apparent is that government officials, business leaders, and community leaders must not only expect but insist that sound business principles be adhered to and that to expect less does more harm than good.

If Blacks and other minorities are to make any progress in the field of business, they must be willing to learn sound business principles and seek partnerships with individuals or firms that offer help for a share of the profits. If both parties have something to lose or gain, they will work harder to make it a success. The Black community must not become caught up in the trap of trying to create a viable business and, at the same time, try to solve the social problems of the community.

Black capitalism may be a nice-sounding slogan, but it has produced very limited results. It has created an atmosphere of hope in some quarters and despair and frustration in others. The program of Black capitalism was initiated to break the cycle of frustration facing Black entrepreneurs, but the evidence shows that the program's efforts have increased the frustrations in both the White and Black communities. The White community asks, what do Blacks want? The Black community feels that business and government efforts are designed to have them fail.

America has the ability to provide to minority groups a share in the free enterprise system. Business realizes that there is an untapped source of manpower and a vast market to be developed in the Black community.

If the Black businessman is to achieve the success of his White counterpart, then the American business community must use all of its knowledge and ability to develop competent Black businessmen. This effort must be motivated out of belief in the free enterprise system and not out of politics or charity.

BIBLIOGRAPHY

Baldwin, James. *Nobody Knows My Name*. New York: A Dell Book, 1964.

Brimmer, Andrew F. and Henry S. Terrell. "The Economical Potential of Black Capitalism." Paper presented before the Eighty-Second Annual Meeting of the American Economic Association, December 29, 1969, New York.

Brown, William H., III. "The EEOC's Chairman Comments on the Persistence of Racism," MBA Journal, Vol. 6, No. 4, January 1972.

Caplovitz, David. *The Poor Pay More*. New York: The Free Press, 1963.

Clark, Kenneth B. "A Psychologist Looks at Discrimination Patterns," *MBA Journal*, Vol. 6, No. 4, January 1972.

Cleaver, Eldridge. *Soul on Ice*. New York: McGraw-Hill, 1968.

Cronon, David. *Black Moses*. Madison: The University of Wisconsin Press, 1969.

Cross, Theodore L. *Black Capitalism*. New York: Atheneum, 1969.

Dunnaville, Clarence M. Jr. and others. "Black Executives: The Darkies at the Bottom of the Stairs," *MBA Journal*, Vol. 3, No. 7, April–May 1969.

Feinberg, Samuel. "Profit, Social Conscience Compatible," *Women's Wear Daily*, January 5, 1971.

Glazer, Nathan and Daniel P. Moynihan. *Beyond the Melting Pot*. Cambridge, Mass.: The MIT Press and Harvard University Press, 1963.

Grier, William H. and Price M. Cobbs. *Black Rage*. New York: Bantam, 1968.

Hagen, Everett E. *The Economics of Development*. Homewood, Illinois: Richard D. Irwin, 1968.

Holmes, Dwight Oliver Wendell. *The Evolution of the Negro University*. New York: Arno Press and *The New York Times*, 1969.

Lee, Roy F. *The Setting for Black Capitalism*. Ithaca, New York: Cornell University Press, In Press.

LeMelle, Tilden J. and Wilbert J. LeMelle. *The Black College*. New York: Frederic A. Praeger Inc., 1969.

Lincoln, C. Eric. *The Negro Pilgrimage in America*. New York: Bantam, 1967.

Lowe, Jeanne R. *Cities in a Race with Time*. New York: Vintage, 1967.

Mays, Benjamin E. and Joseph William Nicholson, *The Black Church*. New York: Russell and Russell Co., 1933.

McKersie, Robert B. "Vitalize Black Enterprise," *Harvard Business Review*, September–October 1968.

Newark News, May 9, 1971.

Piore, Michael J. "Public and Private Responsibilities in On-the-Job Training of Disadvantaged Workers: Department of Econimics Working Paper, Number 23. Cambridge, Massachusetts. The MIT Press, June 1968.

Ross, Arthur M. "The Negro in the American Economy."

Employment, Race, and Poverty, ed. Arthur M. Ross and Herbert Hill. New York: Harcourt, Brace, and World, 1967.

Sturdivant, Frederick D. *The Ghetto Market Place.* New York: The Free Press, 1969.

Tabb, William K. *The Political Economy of the Black Ghetto.* New York: W.W. Norton and Co. Inc., 1970.

The National Advisory Commission on Civil Disorders. "Report of the National Advisory Commission on Civil Disorders." New York: Bantam, 1968.

The Philadelphia Inquirer, July 16, 1970.

The New York Times, March 1, 1970.

The New York Times, April 7, 1972.

The Wall Street Journal, May 1, 1972.

Tuesday Magazine, May 1971.

Wright, Nathan, Jr. *Black Power and Urban Unrest.* New York: Hawthorn Books, 1967.

Yette, Samuel F. The Choice: *The Issue of Black Survival in America.* New York: Berkley Medallion Books, 1972.

About the Author

Charles G. Wells was raised in the town of Ambler, located in Montgomery County, Pennsylvania—about thirty-five miles north of Philadelphia. Ambler has a population of about 6,400 residents and is called the "Asbestos Capital of the World"! It earned that title because of the Keasbey Mattison Company's plant that manufactured asbestos pipes.

Upon graduation from Ambler High School in 1954, the author was accepted at Morgan State University, a HBCU institution located in Baltimore, Maryland. One of the reasons that he wanted to attend Morgan State was that a young lady who was like his big sister, Laura Wilson, and her brother, Larry, were students there. They and their parents had always treated him like family, and his parents knew that they would look out for him and keep him focused. They are still "family" to this day.

As a young brother leaving the small town that he grew up in, having his sister there to watch over him made the transition easier. The friends that he made at Morgan back then, those of them that are left, are still friends today.

Unfortunately, he developed some health issues while at Morgan and had to transfer to a school closer to his hometown. He ended up at Cheyney State College, another HBCU institution. While at Cheyney, he had to drop out because he ended up in the hospital for a two-year stay.

His parents, family, and friends helped him get through those two years by encouraging him and keeping his spirits up. During this very trying period, the support shown to him and his family helped them not to lose faith. This period of his life prepared him for the task and positions that he would hold in the future.

Upon his release from his two-year stay in the hospital being treated for tuberculosis, his parents made sure that he went back to Cheyney State College. They knew that his health issues would necessitate him getting an education.

While at Cheyney, he was able to fulfill his dream of becoming a member of Kappa Alpha Psi Fraternity. His "big sister's" brother and a lot of his childhood friends who'd entered college were members of this fraternity.

He received his MBA from Pace University in New York. His time and the support he received from the faculty at Pace prepared him for the jobs he held in the future.

The events described here impacted his life and played an important part in shaping who he is today. When he was in the hospital—at his lowest point—he received a telephone call from a young lady who would become his wife. That call was the key element that changed the trajectory of his health. She encouraged him to get well and kept him positive in his fight to regain my health.

It was the reason that he was able to accomplish the following in his life to become an international marketing and business consultant. Achieve a career of over sixty-four years of experience working in the public and private sectors in the areas of finance, business and trade in the international arena, and finance, mental health, education and economic and social development in the US.

Mr. Wells has worked in forty-two US states, twenty-three African countries, the Philippines, and Mexico. This former bank president was fortunate to receive Presidential Appointments in two US administrations.